Baseball Backstage

BASEBALL BACKSTAGE

George Sullivan

Holt, Rinehart and Winston
New York

The author is grateful to the New York Yankees for their support of this project. Special thanks are due to Joe Safety and his assistants, Lou D'Ermilio and Anne Melio, for their cooperation.

Published by Holt, Rinehart and Winston,
383 Madison Avenue, New York, New York 10017.
Published simultaneously in Canada by Holt, Rinehart
and Winston of Canada, Limited.

Library of Congress Cataloging in Publication Data
Sullivan, George, 1927–
Baseball backstage.
Summary: Profiles twelve individuals, from general
manager to clubhouse attendant, who play key roles in
the day-to-day activities of the New York Yankees
baseball team.
1. New York Yankees (Baseball team)—Biography—
Juvenile literature. [1. New York Yankees (Baseball
team)—Biography] I. Title.
GV865.A1S84 1986   796.357′64′097471 [B]   85-16418
ISBN: 0-03-000758-5   [920]

First Edition

Designer: Victoria Hartman
Printed in the United States of America
1   3   5   7   9   10   8   6   4   2

ISBN 0-03-000758-5

Contents

Introduction

Most people's idea of baseball is represented by the nine players who run out onto the field just before the playing of the national anthem. Or it is typified by a game-winning home run or slick fielding play.

But that's baseball as a sport. The nine players on the field, the others in the dugout, and the coaches and manager are supported by literally hundreds of other individuals who make up the business of baseball.

Some work for the club itself. Some work for the media, for the newspapers or radio and television stations and networks that cover the games. Others work for the stadium concessionaire or the maintenance company in charge of cleaning up the park when the game is over.

This book profiles twelve individuals who play key roles in the day-to-day activities of one baseball team, the New York Yankees. Each represents a different aspect of baseball as a business.

In their own words, these individuals explain the jobs they do and their responsibilities. In so doing, they're bound to increase your understanding and appreciation of America's most popular sport.

Baseball Backstage

CHAPTER

• 1 •

General Manager

A t the executive level of each baseball club are the owner, or owners—often a board of directors and sometimes a chairman of the board—as well as the team's president and treasurer.

There is also the general manager. It is he who supervises and serves as a link between top management and those responsible for day-to-day operations. The general manager's job is a highly complex one, involving everything from scouting and signing players to ticket selling and stadium management. He is ultimately responsible for media and community relations in addition to player development and the minor leagues. No baseball job is more important.

A general manager's ability in directing the operations of a ball club is usually easy to evaluate. All one has to do is turn to the sports pages of a daily newspaper and look for the column headed "Standings of the Teams." The best general managers run teams that are at the top of their respective divisions, or at least close to the top.

It almost always follows that a team that does well on the field is also among the leaders from a financial standpoint. There are lines at the ticket windows and concession stands. Television ratings shoot up. The result is usually a rosy profit picture.

Affable Clyde King, fifty-nine, with forty years of baseball experience, seven of them as a major league pitcher, signed a five-year contract early in 1984 to serve as general manager of the New York Yankees. But he did so with the understanding that he could return to his hometown of Goldsboro, North Carolina, each year from October to the following February. This shouldn't imply that this is a vacation period for him. October is a busy time of the year. Certain players, by virtue of clauses in their contracts, must be signed by October 15, and others by October 30. So even while at home King is negotiating.

Following that, there is the reentry draft of free agents early in November. Baseball's winter meetings come during the first week in December, and King and his top staff members must attend. Then, after Christmas and New Year's, it's suddenly time to start thinking about spring training.

King was born and brought up in Goldsboro, and he and his wife raised their three daughters there. He was a sophomore at the University of North Carolina when, in 1944, he was signed by the Brooklyn Dodgers.

King's best year with the team was 1951, when he posted a 14–7 record. That was the year the Dodgers lost their $13\frac{1}{2}$–game lead to the Giants. In the ninth inning of the final playoff game, they succumbed to Bobby Thomson's three-run homer against Ralph Branca in the Polo Grounds. King's arm was hurting that day. Otherwise, it would have been he, not Branca, who faced Thomson.

Still plagued by a sore arm the following year, 1952, King finished with a 2–0 record. He was traded to the Cincinnati Reds in 1953, where he finished out his pitching career. His total record: 32 wins, 25 losses.

After that King managed in the minor leagues. But he was back in the majors in 1969 as manager of the San Francisco Giants, and the team finished in second place. During the early 1970s, King was with the Atlanta Braves, first in the front office and later as a field manager.

King joined the Yankees in 1976. He served the New York team as a scout, pitching coach, and manager before taking over as general manager.

Yankee general manager, Clyde King.
(*New York Yankees*)

Someone once said that the first concern of a general manager is "to put a good ball club on the field." Do you agree with that?

I never thought of it in those terms, but off the top of my head, I'd say that was true. To put a good club on the field— that's number one.

Of course, having a team with the right attitude is important, too. But if you've got the right team, you've got the right attitude.

What do you mean by the "right attitude"?
The winning spirit, that's what I mean.

What do you think is the best way to build a good team, a winning team?
I think we should get young players, develop our own young players. We should depend on our farm system as a source of talent. This means beginning with the scouts who find the prospects and having the coaches and managers who can teach them at every level.

Of all the people and departments that you work with in attempting to build a winning team, some must be more important than others. Which ones are they?
I don't think that there is any doubt that there are two departments more important than any others—player development and scouting. They're of almost equal importance. In fact, if you were trying to choose one over the other, it would be like trying to choose between Babe Ruth and Lou Gehrig. I don't think you could come out wrong in choosing either one of those departments.

But I think the scouting department has a little bit of an

edge. You can have the best player-development people and best instructors in the world, but if the scouting department doesn't bring in the best players, it's not doing to do any good. So for that reason I put the scouting department a notch ahead of the player-development department in importance.

I know you rely heavily on the philosophy of having the Yankees develop their own players, on scouting, instruction, and efficient operation at the minor league level. But what about signing free agents? How do you feel about that?

I've always believed that we should sign as few free agents as possible. Mr. Steinbrenner knows my feelings on that. And he's put together some pretty good clubs here by signing free agents. No one could argue with that. But I think we should develop our own players.

However, if a free agent is available, and you can get him, and you think he'll help you, then I'm not averse at all to signing him. But if there's the slightest doubt that the free agent might not help, I'd be willing to take a chance on making a trade or going with the younger players we have.

According to figures from the Major League Baseball Players' Association, the Yankees pay the highest salaries in baseball. In 1984, the average Yankee salary was $458,544. Is that bothersome to you?

I'm all for players getting what they deserve, and even a little more. But not *ten times* as much. I'm not so sure it does the players any good to get a lot more money than they're worth.

I know over the course of the last three or four years that several players, not just one or two, have said to me that they've gotten more money in their negotiations than they thought they would get. (None of these players were our players. I don't think our players would say that to me. They were players on other teams.)

I'm all for the players. I was a player myself. In my position now, I try to be fair to both sides. My first concern, of course, is to the Yankees, to the organization. But I have a concern for the players also.

What qualities do you look for in a field manager?

That's easy. I've had every job you can have in baseball, except owning a club, and I'm not looking forward to that. I enjoy things too much this way.

Getting the very most out of his players—that's the single most important thing. That means getting each player to accept his role, whether it be as a part-time player or as a regular. It means being able to take a player out of the lineup at times, and to give him a rest, and to have that player understand and agree with him, and not pout. It means getting the players to perform up to their capabilities.

That doesn't mean that I don't think that strategy in the field and changing pitchers and things like that aren't important. Those things are super-important. But getting the most out of the players—that's primary in my opinion.

The manager and the general manager have to be close, close enough to know what one another is thinking, so they can agree or disagree, even be able to create something positive out of disagreement.

Suppose we picked twenty-four guys in the spring, and we had two guys who were vying for that twenty-fifth spot on the twenty-five-man roster. And we disagreed on who that twenty-fifth guy might be. I believe the manager should have the final say in a case like that. Absolutely, I do—because I've been a manager and a general manager. I certainly wouldn't insist that my wishes be upheld in a case like that. But I think in order to be able to do that without having a real breakdown in communications, you've got to be close to the manager.

During the season when there's a home game, what is your average day like? What time do you arrive at the park? What time do you leave?

Oh, gosh, it's a long day. But I'm a workaholic; I don't mind work. During the season, I usually get into the office between eight-forty-five and nine o'clock in the morning. In the case of a night game, it's at least midnight before I get home.

What are some of the things you do during the day?

The first thing I do is check the games of the previous day, first in our league and second in the National League. I check to see who's doing well. I try to read all the box scores and accounts of the games. This gives me some of the information I need if we're talking trades with anybody. I check to see what certain hitters are doing against certain pitchers, who's hitting the good pitchers and who isn't, and things like that.

Woody Woodward [vice-president of baseball administration and assistant to the general manager] and I sit down early in the day and decide what we're going to do, and then we go to work on it. I've got a pad that says THINGS TO DO TODAY, and I go over the things that are listed on the pad.

I answer correspondence and I take telephone calls. During the season, I get calls constantly. I hear from other general managers. Sometimes they're just touching base with me. Or one will say to me, "We talked about this guy last week; are you still interested in him?" And I'll say, "No, my interest has cooled. But I've got somebody else *you* might want." Things like that.

And every day I have a meeting with my baseball people. We meet at midafternoon—after everybody has had a chance to get all the game reports from the minor league clubs, determine who won and who lost, who's doing well.

This meeting includes Woody Woodward, Bobby Hofman, director of player development, Doug Melvin, director of scouting, and their assistants. We talk about the games of the previous day, and we spell out what we want to do that day.

Do you watch the ball game?
Oh, *definitely*. I watch every pitch, if possible.

Do you hear from young men and women who are seeking front-office jobs with the Yankees?
That's one of the toughest parts of my job—receiving job applications and not having jobs available for qualified people. It's difficult to get a job in baseball because there are so few of them.

Since I took over the job as Yankee general manager, I've heard from just about everybody I know in baseball. In the first several months I was in this job, my job-application folder grew to be two and a half inches thick. I answer every letter. I don't let one go unanswered.

When I took this job, I told Mr. Steinbrenner one of my objectives would be to have what I call job continuity, getting people trained like we want them, and then keeping them over the years, so we've got a continuity here of knowing each other, knowing how we feel and how we work. So if I happened to be out of the office and was unavailable for a couple of hours, and something important came up, Woody Woodward would know me and know my thinking well enough so he could answer the question or make the decision. That's my point in job continuity.

Do you have any advice for job seekers?
Just keep trying. That's the only advice I have.

CHAPTER

· 2 ·

Director of Scouting

Back in the 1950s, a scout for the Chicago White Sox, Hugh Alexander, signed a young pitcher in Oklahoma named Bruce Swango for $4,000. Then someone from the Baltimore Orioles came along and offered Swango $35,000, not knowing what he had received from the White Sox.

Alexander called his boss, Frank Lane, and told him that he had grown to like the kid and wanted to release him from his Chicago contract so he could accept the Baltimore money.

"Isn't he worth thirty-five thousand dollars?" Lane asked.

"No," said Alexander. "He can't pitch in front of crowds."

If you check *The Official Encyclopedia of Baseball* today, there's no one named Swango listed, testimony to the soundness of Alexander's scouting judgment.

Scouting, which comes down to judging raw baseball talent, is not easy. You can establish how well a young player can run and throw and evaluate his other physical qualities. But his emotional makeup, that's another story. "What's inside him, what he's made of, that type of thing is very tough to project," says Doug Melvin, director of scouting for the New York Yankees.

Melvin, from Chatham, Ontario—"The home of Ferguson Jenkins," he points out—signed with the Pittsburgh Pirates in 1972, when he was twenty. He went to the Yankees three years later as a minor league player and pitched in the Yankee organization for four years. After his release as a player, Melvin became the team's batting-practice pitcher and, during games, manned the walkie-talkie system from the press box to help position Yankee outfielders. He later was in charge of the team's computer operations. He became the director of scouting in 1984.

Scouting has changed a great deal over the past fifteen or so years. One reason for this is the Major League Scouting Bureau, formed in 1974 to help cut costs by eliminating duplication of effort. The bureau, which employs about forty scouts, supplies all clubs with computerized reports on virtually every player in the June draft. During the week the draft is in session, major league general managers and scouting directors select players from a pool of about one thousand high school and college amateurs. About one out of every ten of these players winds up in the major leagues.

This means that a scout today rarely uncovers a player he can point to as his own "find." Nevertheless, scouts continue to play a critical role in any team's success. Not only are they involved in seeking out raw talent, but they are also used more and more to scout rival teams, pinpointing strengths and weaknesses.

How many scouts do you have?
First of all, we have three supervisory scouts who are in charge of certain areas of the country—Gary Hughes, based in Novato, California, Fred Ferreira in Fort Lauderdale, Florida, and Bill Livesay in Ringwood, New Jersey.

Doug Melvin handles scouting operations for the Yankees.
(*George Sullivan*)

The supervisors are in contact with the other scouts we have in the area. They'll also go around and look at players. The supervisor goes through all the players that have high grades from the bureau and our own scouts, and looks at them. He gives a second opinion. He can also be called a cross-checker.

After the supervisory scouts, we have our area scouts, our regular scouts. We have approximately twenty full-time guys and fifteen part-time guys. Most guys have two states to cover, maybe two and a half states. It depends upon the geographical section of the country.

There are bird dogs, too, aren't there? What's a bird dog?

Bird dogs are scouts that work for the area scouts. We call them associate scouts. A bird dog is somebody who will go to the local high school or college games. He's not on salary, not even expenses or anything.

How many different players do your scouts seriously consider in any given year?

In the June draft, you're probably talking thirty-five or forty rounds, and since there are twenty-six teams, you're talking about a thousand players. And that's not counting the players who don't get drafted. You've got to know at least a little bit about each one and a lot about the high-round choices.

How does the work of the Yankee scouts dovetail with that of the scouts that represent the Major League Scouting Bureau?

What we get from the bureau is leads. It's like having somebody go first through an area, screening the players out. Once we have the bureau reports, we can go out and work.

When scouting a young player, what physical qualities does a scout look for?

Two of the main things have always been the ability to run and throw. Those seem to be the two things, no matter how hard you work, you can't improve.

Say a guy runs the hundred-yard dash in thirteen seconds. There's no way he's ever going to get that down to ten seconds, no matter how hard he works.

Or say a guy throws a ball at the speed of eighty miles an hour. There's no way he can improve that to ninety miles an hour.

The other things you can improve upon. But the ability to run and throw, you can't improve upon. That's why you have to look for them first.

What about hitting and hitting with power? Aren't those important too?
You can improve your hitting by continually taking batting practice. Or there may be some flaws in your swing that maybe a hitting coach can help you overcome.

What about fielding?
You have coaches that can help you field. You can also improve your fielding by taking one hundred fifty ground balls a day.

Are pitchers easier to scout than other players?
It depends on the scout. Certain scouts can scout pitchers better than others. Others are better at scouting hitters.
It goes back to the position the scout played as a kid or in professional baseball. Take Bob Lemon [who won 207 games as a pitcher for the Cleveland Indians in the 1940s and 1950s]. He's excellent in scouting pitchers. He can scout others, too, but if you're looking for an opinion on pitchers, you have to go with Bob Lemon. Clyde King [a former Dodger pitcher, now the Yankee general manager] is also outstanding when it comes to pitchers.
Bob Nieman was a pretty good hitter when he played. [In twelve seasons in the major leagues, Nieman compiled a lifetime average of .295.] Bob Nieman can tell a good hitter; he's got an eye for it.

What about evaluating a young prospect from an emotional or psychological standpoint?

That's what's tough, finding out whether baseball is number one to him. And whether he is able to accept bad games, defeat, that kind of thing.

A lot of these kids have always been successful. And then they go to the pro level—and have a bad season. Some kids can't cope with that.

You also have to find out whether the kid is able to pitch in front of big crowds, or when the pressure is on. That stuff is very tough to project.

So what do you do?

My feeling is that the more times you get out to see a kid, the better you're able to read him. And you observe him from the time he arrives at the ballpark. You see whether he comes by himself or whether his father brings him.

And you see what time he gets to the park. Is he ready a half hour before the game or does he get there five minutes before? All of these things mean something.

Is there any advantage for a scout to know other scouts? Isn't there information about prospects that can be obtained from one's rivals?

I sort of lean the other way. I prefer someone who just goes and watches the game and gives his opinion of somebody. I don't particularly go for the guy who introduces himself and sits around with all the other scouts—that type of thing.

When you do that, you hear other people say something about the kid you're watching. Now your mind isn't set on what you thought of him. And you really don't know if the other scout is giving you an honest opinion of the kid, or whether he's talking through his hat.

The scouts that sit together get to peeking over each other's shoulders at one another's radar guns. You might think, *This kid's throwing pretty good*, and then you look over at someone else's gun and the guy says, "Oh, he only threw eighty-two miles an hour on the gun." And that changes your mind.

But how do you know? Maybe the gun wasn't working.

So I like the scout who sits by himself and looks at the player, and judges him. There are other guys who try to get every little bit of information out of every other scout. The only trouble is you don't know whether it's good or bad information. You have got to become a scout of the scout.

Does a scout get better as he gains experience?

It depends. Being a scout is something like being a player. A player has to work on his weaknesses. So does a scout. If a scout knows that he's weak in scouting pitchers, he should work to improve.

It means doing a lot of homework. Suppose there were ten pitchers that he didn't like in the June draft, but they got drafted high. The scout should follow those ten pitchers for the next three or four years. Maybe his opinions were right. But if he was wrong in each case, he should find out why and should ask himself, "Why didn't I like that guy?"

In 1977, when the Yankees beat the Dodgers in the World Series, four games to two, many observers said the New York players were helped a great deal by a secret seven-page scouting report. Six pages were devoted to Dodger hitters and their tendencies and one page evaluated Dodger pitchers. Do you still do that type of scouting?

Sure. That's advance scouting, or major league scouting. We have five full-time major league scouts.

One is Bob Nieman. He goes ahead of the Yankee ball club. If the club is playing Baltimore next week, he goes ahead and sees Baltimore for three or four games before we play them.

And he'll send a report to the manager on the first day we play Baltimore. It will be on injuries, who's hot and cold, and who is going to be pitching in the series—things like that.

If you're in a pennant race in the middle of August, you send scouts out to cover the four or five National League clubs that could possibly be in the Series. You'll get four or five weeks of coverage on each club.

What is a typical day like?
I'm at the office at Yankee Stadium at nine-thirty. I read all the scouting reports that come in. Since I have to be familiar with all the players, that's a lot of reading.

Most of the phone calls have to be completed before twelve o'clock because that's when the scouts go out to see games. In the afternoon, I get very few calls because everyone should be out at a ball game. If I get a phone call from someone, I have to wonder whether it snowed or something.

A scout may call me to make sure it's okay to go and see a prospect when it involves a lot of travel, takes three or four hours, say. I might know whether the guy is still scheduled to play, whether the game has been cancelled or not.

Or maybe I'll call a guy because I heard some kid, who we think to be a high prospect, is going to work out. I heard it through the grapevine or read it in the paper or something. I just give the scout a call to make sure he gets to the workout.

There's really no need to call very often. The scouts should be out there.

Do people write to you and suggest players to the Yankees based on scouting they've done, people who are not affiliated with baseball?
That happens a lot. When it happens, I find out where the

prospect lives, and I send the letter to the scout in that area. Suppose someone writes and says there is this kid in New Jersey and he is an All-League second baseman in such and such a school. I just put the letter in the mailbox of Joe DiCarlo, our New Jersey scout, and leave it up to him to look up the kid.

Every area of the country is pretty well scouted. There are few players that are missed.

Do you hear from people who would like to be employed as scouts?

We get all kinds of letters from guys who want scouting jobs. We have to send back form letters saying we don't have openings.

Whenever you're looking for a job in baseball, the first thing they ask is whether you played the game. That applies to scouting. If you've never played the game, they'll say, "How can you scout?"

It's the same as if I was to apply for a banking job. I have no banking background, so it would be very difficult for me to get a job. Baseball is like that. If you haven't played the game, it's tough to get hired.

·3·

Director of
Player Development

O nce a scout signs a prospect, he is placed with a minor league team that is appropriate for the young man's ability and experience. Minor league teams range in classes of ability from AAA, the highest, to Rookie League, the lowest.

At the time the 1985 baseball season opened, the Yankees' minor league teams included:

Team	League	Classification
Columbus Clippers	International	AAA
Albany-Colonie Yankees	Eastern	AA
Fort Lauderdale Yankees	Florida State	A
Oneonta Yankees	New York–Pennsylvania	A
Greensboro Hornets	South Atlantic	A
Sarasota Yankees	Gulf Coast	Rookie

Bobby Hofman, fifty-eight, a baseball veteran whose career has covered almost four decades, directs minor league operations for the New York team. From St. Louis, Hofman has done about everything in baseball but sell tickets. He was a utility infielder and catcher with the Giants in the National League for seven seasons in the years just before the club moved to San Francisco. (In 341 times at bat, he hit .248.) He managed in the minor leagues. He was a major league coach. He was a director of farm-team operations, as well as a scouting director. "I've done a little of everything," he says.

As director of player development, how do you describe what you do?

My job is to keep track of each player in our minor league system, working with our coaches and managers to evaluate them, and eventually decide which ones we should recommend as major league prospects.

We try to establish whether a prospect is a "Yankee type"

Minor league director Bobby Hofman (*left*) works closely with scouting director Doug Melvin.
(*George Sullivan*)

of ballplayer—a winning ballplayer. We have a winning tradition.

New York is a tough place to play, perhaps the toughest in the country. Especially in Yankee Stadium. People expect you to play great all the time. They don't want to see you make any mistakes.

The Yankees have got to win. If we don't win, attendance falls tremendously. People are all over the ballplayers, all over the management. In other towns you can play only half decently and people don't get all over you. They're still rooting for you.

So that's your overall goal, to develop major league ball-players with a winning attitude?

That's right. My overall goal is to have everyone we sign play in the major leagues. But you can't possibly do that. So our number-one goal is to win everywhere we have a minor league ball club.

Of course, the main thing is for the Yankees to win. We try to help them in any way we can from our supply of minor league players. Or we try to give the organization good players that we can *trade* for ballplayers who can help the team win.

But doesn't that set up a conflict with the minor league clubs? When you bring up star players to the Yankees or trade them away, doesn't it affect your relationship with the fans in the minor league city? Don't they get upset?

No, no; it doesn't happen. We have a very good relationship with our clubs because we win. We've been winners.

We might take a ballplayer away from a club during the regular season, but we try not to make a practice of it. And we never take players from a minor league team when that team is involved in play-off competition.

If [Rex] Hudler is playing at Columbus and [Willie] Randolph [the Yankee second baseman] gets hurt, we might bring Hudler up. We'll then take the next best second baseman from, maybe, Albany and bring him up to Columbus—so it's a chain reaction.

Another thing. Columbus fans love to see Columbus players come up with the Yankees and do well. They love it because they're always identified as having played at Columbus.

How many players are you and your managers and coaches involved with?

We take about a hundred sixty-five players to spring training. Maybe we end up with a hundred twenty-five. They will all be put on different rosters.

We'll sign maybe thirty more players in June—at the draft. So we'll end up dealing with a hundred ninety-five to two hundred players for the year.

How do you keep track of so many players?

After a game is played, every minor league manager telephones in a report. It's recorded by an answering machine. The next morning a written transcript is made.

In his report, the manager evaluates his pitcher for the game. He also evaluates some players, but not all players. If someone made a good play, it's mentioned in the report. Errors, stolen bases, attempted steals—things like that—are in the report.

I also talk to every minor league manager every day. We talk about individual players. How is this fellow going? How's that one going? We especially talk about the player who might be in a little bit of trouble, not playing up to expectations. We'll try to establish what's happening with the kid.

For instance, we might see in a box score that a kid went oh for four. The manager will explain how the kid hit the ball; he might have had four line drives.

It's usually the manager that I talk with, but sometimes the pitching coach calls me or I call the pitching coach.

Some of the players are quite young, aren't they, just out of high school. Does this present any special problem?

You're talking about the players we sign at the June draft. We might place some of them with the Rookie League at Sarasota or with our Onconta team, which is class A.

This is the first year most of these kids have been away from home. We just want them to get their feet on the floor.

The managers and coaches at those teams try to help the kids. "If you've got any problems, come to us," they say. "Let us try to help you."

A high school kid goes home, he knows a meal is going to be on the table that night. He knows he's going to have a clean shirt in the morning. Well, a kid going to Sarasota doesn't know that. He has to go out and get a meal. He's got to make sure his clothes get washed. He's away from home. He's playing ball every night. Instead of going to bed at ten-thirty or eleven, when the family might have gone to bed, he now doesn't get through playing until ten-thirty or so. By the time he showers and has a bite to eat, it's twelve-thirty or one o'clock. It's a whole different life.

So the managers and coaches watch the kids. A kid that's losing weight may be having problems. Maybe he's only eating a hot dog every day. Or maybe a kid gains ten pounds. You talk to him. It's like being a mother.

Is there a greater emphasis on instruction in the minor leagues nowadays than there used to be?

I would think so; yes. At one time, most clubs had one minor league pitching coach, a roving coach. He went from one team to another giving instruction.

The Yankees established a policy of having a minor league pitching coach at every level. That is, at every place we have a ball club, we have a pitching coach.

We also have another coach at every club. He can be an infield instructor, a catching instructor, an outfield instructor, or a hitting instructor.

Basically, what the Yankees did was put two coaches at every level—plus the manager. Most clubs had the manager doing everything.

The Baltimore Orioles are said to have an eighty-eight-page handbook that spells out the organization's teaching philosophy. Coaches who instruct players in the minor leagues follow what the handbook says to do. As a result, everyone on every level learns the same method of play. Do the Yankees have a similar handbook?

Everybody in baseball has a basic playbook, how to make this play, how to make that play. Basically they're all the same.

Say on a ground ball hit back to the pitcher. Everybody says don't stand still. You're supposed to take a little crow-hop and throw the ball. Every club teaches the play that way. So Baltimore puts that in their book and says it's the Baltimore way. Well, it's the Yankees' way; it's the Dodgers' way; it's Cincinnati's; it's everyone's way.

Guys may say things differently. For example, one pitching coach may say to "drive" off the mound; another will say to "push" off the mound. But basically it's all the same.

Everything comes from the big club—how you make your relay plays, how you do this, how you do that. It comes from the manager of the Yankee team. Everything is the way he wants it. We do it in the minor leagues the way he wants it done in the major leagues.

Does luck play a part in the advancement of players from the minor leagues to the big leagues?

If you have the ability, I think it will come out. You may miss on your first chance, but if you have the ability, somewhere along the line you're going to play in the big leagues.

Getting your chance—that's what is important, right?

That's the big thing—your chance, your chance to play with the big team.

You have to get your chance. If you don't get your chance, you can never prove you can play up here.

When you do get your chance, you've got to prove yourself. You've got to be ready to do your job.

Joe Cowley is an example. He got his chance. In 1984, he came up here and did an outstanding job. If, in his first three games, he had pitched poorly, he might not have lasted with the Yankees. [Cowley compiled a 9–2 record and a 3.66 ERA during the 1984 season.]

Those two kids at the Mets—Dwight Gooden and Darryl Strawberry. They each got a chance, and they proved they could do it.

Still, moving from the minors to the major leagues is no easy task. Even in the case of your AAA team, the Columbus team, only a small handful of players will ever get to play regularly in the major leagues.

Well, not in the case of the team in 1984. We had [Scott] Bradley catching. We feel he will make it. [Rex] Hudler was playing second base. We expect him to make it. André Robertson was the shortstop. Mike Pagliarulo was the third baseman. There's four guys in the infield we expect to make it.

Then we had [Stan] Javier in the outfield. That makes five. [Brian] Dayett came up eventually. We had six or seven guys on the club that we expected to make it. Eventually that number could reach eight or ten.

Eight or ten will eventually make it to the majors? That's exceptional, isn't it?

It was an exceptional year.

Nevertheless, a minor league player with a AAA club, while he's very close to a major league job, is still very far away. It's a big step.

It is a big step. But you're only a heartbeat away. You know what I mean? If something happens to Willie Randolph, you're suddenly looking for a second baseman.

CHAPTER

• 4 •

Head Trainer

What is a baseball club, after all, but simply a collection of individuals with special physical capabilities? In recent years, as the cost of employing these specialists has shot upward—the average salary of a Yankee player in 1984 was $458,544—so, too, has the importance of the individual who cares for them—the trainer.

The trainer is with the team every day. He works closely with and is supervised by the team physician, determining those injuries or illnesses that require the physician's diagnosis and treatment. He then carries out the physician's instructions in treating players.

The trainer ministers first aid when an injury occurs. He's involved in the rehabilitation of muscle injuries. He's concerned about the prevention of injuries and the general health of the players. He makes recommendations concerning each player's diet and weight.

The importance of the trainer is underscored by the enormous array of equipment at his disposal. Within the trainer's rooms, located just off the team's dressing room, are two whirlpool baths, big metal tubs in which either hot or cold water circulates rapidly. There is an ultrasonic machine, which converts electrical energy to mechanical energy within a tissue by means of high-frequency sound waves that increase circulation in the tissue.

There's a hydrocollator, a hot-pack machine. This provides moist-heat applications for large muscle areas, for shoulder, arm, or leg muscles. Hot packs are used to relieve stiffness or soreness, or even headaches.

There are several metal treatment tables. On these, players stretch out to be massaged.

There is also likely to be traction equipment to forestall muscle spasms in the neck, a machine to provide electrical muscle stimulation, and a paraffin bath for the hands and fingers or ankles or feet. There are vibrators to stimulate deep muscle areas. There are cabinets, trunks, and storerooms filled with medical supplies.

In baseball's ragtag days, the trainer often got his job because he was a friend of the manager or owner. His medical background scarcely qualified him to treat a hangnail. Not anymore. Major league baseball now requires that trainers be certified by the National Athletic Trainers Association (NATA).

The certification requirements include a four-year Bachelor of Science degree from a college offering the proper courses, those in physiology (the science dealing with the functions of the human body), injury care and prevention, and drugs and medication. A minimum amount of on-the-job training is also required.

The trainer must also pass a certification examination—written, oral, and practical, which is known to be very tough. Even after he's certified, the trainer has to keep up-to-date by taking additional training courses each year.

Gene Monahan, head trainer for the New York Yankees, has not only been thoroughly trained, he has plenty of experience.

His career began in the early 1960s. "I was a junior in high school and batboy for the Fort Lauderdale Yankees in my hometown of Fort Lauderdale, Florida," he recalls, "and one day the equipment man quit, so I took over the clubhouse.

"The next year, after I had graduated, they asked me whether I'd like to become a trainer, and I said yes."

For the next ten years Gene worked in the Yankees' minor league system, edging his way upward. He worked for the Fort Lauderdale Yankees for two years; the Columbus Yankees in Columbus, Georgia, for two years; the Binghamton Triplets, a former Yankee farm team, in Binghamton, New York, for two years; and the Syracuse Chiefs in Syracuse, New York, a triple-A team, for four years. During four of those ten years— from 1965 through 1969—he studied professional athletic training at the University of Indiana, where he received his degree.

Married, the father of two young daughters, Gene and his family rent a home in Little Ferry, New Jersey. "I would prefer to live in the South," he says, "but this is a twelve-months-a-year job."

In the case of a home game, what time do you start work?

Night games at home begin at eight-oh-five P.M. I pick up my assistant, Mark Letendre, at two o'clock in the afternoon, or he picks me up, and we drive to the ballpark. It takes a half-hour or so.

There's always something waiting for you. Even if you didn't leave the ballpark until midnight the previous day, there's always something on the desk—phone calls or mail—that has to be taken care of.

We get a lot of medical bills that have to be screened and approved. We get mail from people who want advice. They're people in the field, related friends, or, simply, fans. "What do

Monahan (*extreme left*) spends each game in the dugout. Players pictured are (*left to right*) Dave Righetti and Ron Guidry, plus coach Don Zimmer. (*Louis Requena*)

I do for this?" they want to know. "What do I do for that?" A father will write and say, "My son is a pitcher; he's fifteen. What kind of conditioning program should he be on?" We answer such mail if and when we get the time.

We spend about a half-hour a day checking our medical supplies and ordering what's needed. And we also have to check the medical trunks, the four trunks we take with us on the road. We make sure the supplies in the trunks get replenished.

We get the machines heated that we feel we're going to need for physical therapy that day. We fill the whirlpools.

Around three-thirty or four o'clock, the players start drifting in and we start treatments. We also bring players into the office to discuss treatments or programs.

Each day I have to spend twenty or thirty minutes with the manager. We discuss who can play and who can't. We talk about what we might be able to do to get a guy in there.

I also spend time talking with the coaches about certain players. And occasionally I'm called upstairs to speak to the general manager or owners.

What is your schedule like in the hours before the game?
The players have to be out of the training room at five-thirty. That's when the team has to go out onto the field. No one is allowed in the training room after five-thirty, except the starting pitcher, who is resting, or someone who is hurting and cannot perform.

The nine players who are starting that night take batting practice at six o'clock. So some of these players may get special attention between five-thirty and six.

After taking batting practice, the team comes back into the clubhouse, and then we have another thirty or forty minutes to work with them, time for some final leg or arm stretches. There may be some applications of ointments or oils that we make up, or commercial products. These help to keep the players warm and loose.

We prepare the starting pitcher at seven or seven-fifteen for an eight-oh-five game. I'll massage him to relax him and then I'll stretch him. Then maybe I'll massage his elbow and shoulder—get him ready for the game. About half of our pitchers request this preparation.

At seven-forty-five or so we shut down the training room and change into our clothes—white pants and dark blue top. We're in the dugout at eight o'clock.

What are your responsibilities during the game?
We sit by the manager or one of the coaches. We don't leave

his side unless one of us has to run an errand, go to the training room for something.

You have to observe the field. You have to be aware of what's happening in the dugout between innings. You have to keep an eye on the pitcher at all times.

We're on the bench for the entire game. We have to have certain paraphernalia out there with us. We have a medical kit, an on-the-field kit, an ice chest, sunglasses for the players (if it's a day game), a gum box (so the players have their favorite chewing gum available), and a Gatorade cooler with the flavor of the day—orange, lemon-lime, or fruit punch. We rotate them, but if the starting pitcher happens to like a certain flavor, he gets it.

What happens once the game is over?

Our games usually end around eleven o'clock. We're in the training room until eleven-forty-five or so, involved in post-game care. Then we have a schedule we follow that involves cleaning our training rooms and whirlpool rooms.

We leave the ballpark around twelve-thirty. I'm usually home by twelve-forty-five or one o'clock.

Once in a while it gets a little tough, like when you get home at one o'clock and you have to get up at seven-thirty the same morning for a day game. For a day game, we have to be at the park at about nine-thirty. The players have to be dressed at noon for a two-oh-five game.

Are road games tougher or easier for you?

On road trips, you get a break. We still get to the ballpark at two or two-thirty as we do at home, but because our team takes batting practice after the home team, we don't start getting busy until much later.

Usually we take the injured players to the ballpark in a cab.

We don't have the facilities we have available at Yankee Stadium, which can cause problems. For instance, at the Stadium I have two whirlpools and four treatment tables. But on the road I may have only one whirlpool and two treatment tables. You have to get the guys that require a lot of time out of the way by the time the bus arrives at the stadium with the whole team. Otherwise, you've got a mess of guys all wanting something at once. They get on each other's nerves. And the manager gets upset when they're not ready for batting practice. It's our job to get the players out early.

As a trainer, you get free time on the road in the morning. You either can catch up on your sleep or maybe you do some shopping for your ball club. Suppose we're on a ten-day road trip and you get a rash of colds and sore throats. Well, I might run a little short on lozenges and throat swabs and sprays. Or I might want to have the team gargle with a mixture of certain things. So I have to go shopping for what I need.

What supplies do you take with you when you travel?
We have four trunks. One trunk is mostly medications and topical creams and ointments, plus bottles of liniments and the like that we make up.

Another trunk is medical supplies covering the eye and ear; allergies; blood pressure equipment; stethoscopes; units for nerve stimulation; fungal sprays; sunglass-repair equipment; extra sunglasses; plus other paraphernalia.

The third large trunk is wraps and splints, sweatbands, and bulk equipment we need, much like a football club would have. There are a lot of Ace bandages, splinting materials, casting materials, foam rubber, and things of that nature.

The fourth trunk contains various kinds of tape. Vitamins are in that trunk, too.

Plus I'll carry a little medical bag. It's with me all the time.

It contains a conglomeration of small items, pills, ointments, different kinds of medications. It has a lot of things you need on the spur of the moment—ammonia capsules, cotton-tipped applicators, tongue blades, flashlight, and some surgical instruments.

I take the bag everywhere. It's at the ballpark. It's in my hotel room, and it's on the plane.

In each town you go to, it's a league rule that the home team has to have certain types of therapeutic equipment available for the visiting team, things we would obviously have a terrible time carrying. In the American League, teams provide a whirlpool bath, an ultrasound machine, and a hydrocollator for one another.

We also provide light weights for rehabilitation work and an ergometer, an exercise bicycle. We do a lot of work with that now.

Before a road trip, we're involved in things like calling ahead to hotels for bedboards for certain players. And before the season, I write the other clubs in the league, explaining what kind of food and drink we want in the clubhouse, and what we don't want. We have to make sure the players' gum is there and their chewing tobacco.

Besides taking care of players' bodies, aren't you also involved with their equipment?

All the time. A rawhide string may snap on a player's glove, for instance. It's the trainer's job to fix it. I learned years ago how to restring a glove. Sometimes I can do it between innings.

When I first started hanging around baseball parks in 1963, Don Seger, who later was head trainer for the Phillies, was my idol. He showed me how to take a needle and restring a glove. Boy, if you could take a guy's glove home at night and do it up for him nice, and he liked it the next day, that was a real plus for you as an apprentice trainer.

But it got out of hand one year at spring training. I was taking home three or four gloves a night. I was getting them all.

Part of the trainer's job is to see to it that playing equipment fits correctly. Sunglasses, for instance. You have to be sure they're safe, padded properly in certain areas, that the lenses are appropriate for the particular sky and that they fit properly.

We also help the players with their selection of shoes. If your feet hurt, it can cause problems in every part of your body.

Do you make recommendations as to what the players eat— or are supposed to eat?

We're not here to feed the players. They're supposed to have their afternoon meal before a night game at home. And it is good to eat three or four hours before the ball game. They're pretty much on their own.

Here at the stadium, we provide a snack of cut-up fruit and fresh, raw vegetables before the game. Plus fruit juices.

After batting practice, we don't serve anything.

After the game, the equipment man will work with the Stadium club or outside people to provide a light, warm meal for the players—if they want it. About half of them do. Sometimes it's a meat loaf sandwich, broiled chicken, or spaghetti, which I really promote.

The meal is not at all elaborate. It's usually a one- or two-item thing. They have a can of beer or a fruit juice or soda. Then it's out the door. I'm not into feeding players at the ballpark.

But if you provide that light stuff here and there you can keep the players from sending the batboys to McDonald's or Wendy's. Because they'll do that. And they'll sneak those burgers and fries in here, although I'm not putting down burgers and fries; they have a lot of nutritional value. But they're not appropriate an hour and a half before a ball game. Afterward, I don't mind it. During the day—great. Sometimes that's all the ballplayers get. Sometimes that's all *I* get. But before a game, you're opening yourself to gastric problems, which we've had in the past.

So we keep it light; we keep it healthy.

When it comes to the care and treatment of injuries, players have to believe in you, trust in you. How do you go about building that trust?

One thing I learned years ago, I don't believe in babying players at all, and we don't. I fight that every year.

But I do try to demonstrate to the players that I'm concerned about them, that I think about them. For example, you might learn that a player likes a certain type of lip balm, and you get him a little jar of it, and you just fire it at him in the dugout. He's real impressed with that. "This guy is doing his homework," he says to himself.

You have to be kind of a psychologist in dealing with the players. Say you're on the bench and there are several guys sitting there who aren't playing that day, so you might pick one out and say to him, "We have an afternoon game tomorrow, and I think you're playing in it, aren't you?"

"Yeh, so what?" he says.

"Well, I notice your eyelashes are getting a bit long. Maybe this evening we could trim those for you. In a day game, with that sweat, you might get some water hanging off them. You never know. A ball goes up and, even though you have flip-down sunglasses, you might get some blurriness there, and you have a problem."

When you do something like that, you know there are three or four guys on either side of him that heard the story, and one or two of them will come in and say, "Hey, what about my eyelashes? You'd better take a look at them."

That's how you get things done.

What about the players' families? Do you get involved with them?

Yes, to a certain degree. When a player feels that you know what you're doing and that you have a good background and work closely with the doctor, he'll trust you to medicate his family. It's a ticklish situation, and I really don't like to do it. And whenever I have to give anything that in any way relates to a prescriptive item, I check with the doctor.

The players ask you to take care of things like family colds and hay fever. We're asked to help in coping with pregnancies. Or when a child is born and the player can't get enough rest. We're asked to give advice.

We had a "baby boom" on the Yankees recently, and players were sometimes coming in cranky, swollen-eyed, and just miserable. "Help me with this," a guy would say. So we'd talk to him about regulating schedules and about how the baby is feeling. You really have to get into it. If the player's wife is breast-feeding, maybe the baby isn't getting enough milk, and you back it up with something that is isotonic in formula.

We've had players come back and say, "Gee, you know that's working; the baby sleeps four hours. And if we get the baby up at one-thirty or two o'clock in the morning, when I'm about ready to go to bed after a tough night game, she sleeps until five-thirty or six. My wife gets up then, and I can sleep until nine-thirty or ten." Those kinds of things you have to work out.

What about your duties and responsibilities once the season is over, once the players have gone back to their hometowns?

At the end of the season, I go over everyone's file—all their reports, the different percentages of body fat each player had, the different body weights, all their daily work, and all the problems they've had—and I do a player profile. The profile helps you to decide what you want to improve.

I try to make it clear and concise so it can be read by the people I work for, the people upstairs. It's primarily for them. It enables them to sit down and say, "This player may have been off for this reason or that reason, and let's try to attack it that way."

Then you go after the player and try to get him to improve the things in which he's weak. You design his program for the winter months. You design what he needs to be doing to stay in shape for spring training.

I utilize our strength and conditioning coach, Jeff Mangold, a real professional. He works directly with the players on conditioning.

In our ball club, when the players come to spring training, they're expected to be in *great* physical condition, a good body weight. We want their body weight down so they can do the work we're going to ask them to do.

If they come to spring training out of shape, they're going to break down. If they can't finish their work, they're going to lose time, and they're going to have problems making the ball club.

Overall, it's in the players' best interests to follow what we want them to do. They don't all do it. But if we get thirty percent of them to do it, we're way ahead of the game. And the other guys, the ones who don't, you just stay after them all winter.

CHAPTER

·5·

Director of
Media Relations

Whenever there is a need for a baseball club to communicate with the press or broadcast media, or whenever a newspaper reporter or broadcaster wants to know something about the club, the media relations director is called upon. He is the link between the club and the communications world.

It's the media relations director who helps to arrange interviews for writers and broadcasters, arranges press conferences to announce signings and other important happenings, oversees the preparation and distribution of the media guide and news releases, and supervises the operation of the press box.

Joe Safety, smart and energetic, is the media relations director for the New York Yankees. Born in Parkersburg, West Virginia, and raised in St. Mary's, a small town north and east of Parkersburg, Safety attended the University of West Virginia, where he earned one degree in sociology and another in public relations.

A third baseman, Safety played two years of baseball while

Safety shares a light moment with John Montefusco and other pitchers at
Yankee training camp.
(*George Sullivan*)

at college. He was good in the field but not notable as a hitter.
"The ball kept getting smaller," he says.

At thirty-two, Safety worked in public relations for the Pittsburgh Pirates from the mid-1970s until 1981, then was out of
baseball for a while. He joined the Yankees early in 1983. "I
came back with the Yankees," he says, "because I missed the
pace, the intensity of baseball. There's nothing like it."

Is there a job description for what you do?
No. And even if there was, you don't have enough tape or
time to get it all down.

*Why is that? What makes the job so complex, so hard to
describe?*

It's because there are an infinite number of things that can happen that can affect how your day goes. Once, when I was at Pittsburgh, and it was the off-season, I was planning a long weekend in the Bahamas. The evening before I was supposed to leave, Willie Stargell was in the backyard of his suburban Pittsburgh home with his pistol (which he was fully licensed to own and use) and he accidentally fired it and the bullet grazed his leg and he went to the hospital.

I felt really badly. Willie Stargell was—and is—a close, close friend of mine. My life has been enriched through my association with him. But he blew my trip to the Bahamas. I spent the entire next day answering questions about Willie's condition, questions that ranged from natural concern for his welfare to those that expressed some hope for a scandal.

I don't know where [Yankee pitcher] Dave Righetti—to just pick a name—is right now. But there's a chance that wherever he is something could happen to him to affect what I do for the rest of the day or tomorrow.

And there are twenty-five Dave Righettis at the major league level, about a couple of hundred in the Yankee organization, and about a thousand former Yankees—and if something happens to any of them, my phone is going to start ringing.

It sounds like you're kind of the point man for the club.

I play a liaison role. That's the simple way to put it. I'm the person who interfaces with the writer and broadcaster. When there's a need for the club to communicate with the media, or vice versa, I should be the conduit.

I know that running the press box is an important part of your job during the season. Tell me about that; what do you try to achieve there?

During the season, when the Yankees are at home, Safety spends much of his time this way.
(*George Sullivan*)

Generally speaking, my people and I try to provide a flow of pertinent information to the media representatives, not too much information, nor too little, a balance.

In my first year with the Yankees, which was my first year in the American League, I remember visiting one stadium where the press-box spokesman picked up the microphone just once during the game, and that was to announce the attendance. Burton Hawkins gave no pitcher's line, announced no milestones, gave no injury report, and announced no lineup changes.

I suppose there are press boxes where the guy running it

never shuts up. He repeats information that's already in writing in front of people.

I'm reasonably pleased with the level we hit. Pertinent information is what I try to provide.

In terms of written information, what does that include?
Our media notes, which are exhaustive. We produce from fourteen to sixteen pages of notes every day there's a game.

We make three hundred copies of each page. That means we turn out from forty-two hundred to forty-eight hundred pages of information daily.

It sounds like you're running a publishing company.
That's right. With deadlines. And with information that is counted upon to be accurate. We're *the* authorities on the New York Yankees.

What do the media notes contain?
The lineups.
The team's record for the season.
Yankee batting and pitching stats for the season.
The visiting team's batting and pitching stats for the season.
The standings in both leagues.
American League batting and pitching statistics.
A capsulized story of the games of every one of our minor league teams from the day before.

Wire-service copy concerning baseball, maybe a commissioner's decision or ruling or an important trade.

The notes also contain a box called "Yankees at a Glance" [see next page] that any writer worth his salt ought to be able to use. It tells you what the team's record is today, what the score was yesterday, the last time the team won, the last time the team lost, the longest winning streak for the season, the longest losing streak, how the team fared over the past five games, over the past ten games, what the team's record was at this time last year, and the team's record, month-by-month, for this season and for the previous season.

Yankees at a Glance
Current Streak: 4 wins
Longest Winning Streak: 4 Games
  (5/6–10; 5/13–16, 7/12–14)
Longest Losing Streak: 5 Games
  (4/30–5/5)
Last 5 Games: 4–1
Last 10 Games: 7–3
Game No.: 87
Home Game No.: 40
Road Record: 17–30
Current Series: 4–0 vs. KC
Last Road Trip: 3–7 (KC, TEX, MINN)
Last Home Stand: 2–1 vs. DET
Last Win: 7/14, 4–1 vs. KC
Last Loss: 7/8, 4–3 @ MINN
86 Game Record, '83: 47–39
37 Game Record, '83: 48–39
April '84: 8–13 . . . April '83: 9–11
May '84: 12–14 . . May '83: 16–10
June '84: 13–14 . . June '83: 14–12
July '84: 7–5 . . . . . July '83: 17–10
Pre All-Star Game: 36–46
Post All-Star Game: 4–0

It takes about five working hours to produce the information for a game. That means that sometime between the last out of one game and the first pitch of the ensuing game, five hours of work has to be done. Our biggest nightmare is a day game after a night game. We hate 'em. We hate 'em at home. We hate 'em on the road. Our people scramble when one occurs. Sometimes they spend their nights here.

After the game, we produce a new set of statistics that includes the game just played. We produce a box score.

We also produce a play-by-play account of the game. One of our people types up what every batter does, what every play is, and every lineup change. At the end of the play-by-play, we type the names of the winning and losing pitchers, the attendance, time of the game, the line score—runs, hits, and errors. We're the only club that provides a play-by-play.

We also provide postgame notes. If there happened to be a note in the material we distributed before the game that said, "Ron Guidry's next strikeout will be the 1,500th of his career," and Ron Guidry gets that strikeout in the second inning, then the postgame notes will say, "Ron Guidry's first strikeout in tonight's game, which occurred against Bob ("Buddy") Bell in the second inning, was the 1,500th of his career."

Our postgame notes might also include such stuff as, "Dave Winfield was forced to leave tonight's game because of a slight pull of the left hamstring."

What are some of the questions you're asked in the press box during a game?

Often, press-box questions concern records. They're questions that begin, "When was the last time . . . ?" Or, "Who was the last Yankee who . . . ?"

Say a guy gets five hits in a game, people then ask, "Has he ever gotten five hits in a game before?" And you have to have the answer.

Sometimes the questions have to do with strategy. A writer who has been covering the club regularly and has gotten a feel for what players are going good or going bad will say, "Why don't you bunt here and move the runner over?" Or "Why don't you pinch-hit here?"

These kinds of things are rhetorical. My answers to such

questions don't mean a thing. The manager gets paid to make those decisions.

For part of the time I was in Pittsburgh, Chuck Tanner was the manager. He is well known as a communicator. Tanner used to do incredibly unorthodox things on the field. Self-proclaimed experts in the press box would cry out, "How can he *do* that?"

"That goes against the book," a writer would say to Tanner.

"But I've never seen this book," Tanner would always answer. "Where is this book?"

What problems do you encounter in running the press box?

There's an age-old problem that exists in this business. It has to do with the fact that the people I have to deal with don't get along together very well. I have to deal with people as clearly different as Diane Sawyer [of CBS's "60 Minutes"] and Dick Young [of the *New York Post*].

The electronic media and the print media are constantly at each other's throats. They have a provincial attitude toward one another. Generally, the print media covers us solidly, consistently. When something is going on at Yankee Stadium that is of interest—an Old Timers Day, for instance—there's an increase in the number of people from the print media that cover the club. But what really changes is that the TV crews come out in droves. And the guys that come here all the time, guys whose equipment consists of a pad and a pencil, are confronted with people carrying tripods and sound equipment and everything.

One side says, "We're not here much, so we should be treated differently when we are here." The other people say, "We're here all the time. Why are they in our way?"

The problem exists all the time, always has, always will.

What else causes you problems?

One of the things that bothers me most is when somebody who has been here every day—if we've played thirty-five games, somebody who has been here thirty-five days—asks me a stupid question, I mean one that can be answered by written information we've already provided, and can be found in the same place every day.

That's laziness as far as I'm concerned. I may take that a little personally.

Do you say something?

Sure. "It's in the notes." That's my standard answer.

What about the players and their relationships with the writers and broadcasters. Does that cause any difficulties for you?

Once in a while. Suppose a writer comes up to me and says, "I'd really like to get a minute with a particular player to morrow during the day."

So I get the player on the phone at his home, and he says, "I'll be available between twelve and one o'clock. Have him call me then."

At two-thirty the person who had wanted to talk to the player calls me and says, "I've been calling him and he hasn't been there."

Then I see the player and say to him, "When you tell *me* you're going to be somewhere, then you'd better be there. Or don't ever come back to me for the things that I know you'll want to come back to me for. You're going to want a photograph; you'll want me to get you a car on the road—these little side things. I'll no longer be available to do these things for you because when you told *me* you'd be home and you weren't there, you made me look bad. My fingerprints were on this thing. Not yours. And you don't have the right to fool with my credibility that way."

That kind of thing happens six or eight times during the season.

It's not always the player's fault. Many times the players have a solid inclination to do what they said they would do. Maybe they didn't actually want to do it, but they said they'd do it. And then the media person comes up short. Well, they get the same talk from me.

Does being in New York make your job different in any way?

There are more newspapers in this market—ten of them—than in other markets. This makes for more competition, more intensity. This means the writers have to dig a little and maybe dig in a different direction.

And only in Chicago and Los Angeles do papers have the kinds of deadlines they have in New York. These guys have deadlines all day long. There is no such thing as a morning or an afternoon paper anymore. The *Daily News*, the *Times*, the *Post*, and the *Newark Star-Ledger* come out all day.

This means that if I get a piece of information to the writer for the *Daily News* at two o'clock, and not to the writer for the *Post* by three o'clock, the *Post* is going to have the information in one less edition than the *News*. And these guys take that real personally—because their publishers take it personally, and their readers take it personally. "How come the *Post* didn't have this trade?" they want to know. "It was in the *Daily News*." That's the responsibility we have to live with here.

Do you feel that you have any real influence on the media, that is, do you have an effect upon what is written and what is said about your team?

I'm a realistic guy. I really don't think you're supposed to say the Yankees are good when you know they're bad. I don't think you should go out of your way to say they're bad when they're good.

I think the business is, you see what you see, and you form some perception about it, and you relate it to a huge amount of people. You're giving them an assessment of what has taken place.

Fairness and accuracy are all I'm looking for. I don't care about enhancement. I don't care about spiciness. I don't care about dirt. I don't care what happens outside the white lines. I'm mostly interested that the general public gets a fair and accurate account of what happens here. If it also happens to be entertaining and positive, that's fine.

I'm not in the business of trying to editorially manipulate people. If someone says to me that their assessment of a situation is such that it is not going to reflect well on the Yankees, I can't take issue with it—as long as it's fair and accurate.

What time does your working day begin; what time does it end?

The players just don't show up at seven-thirty in the evening, put on their uniforms, and go out and play at eight o'clock. Players come to work at four or four-thirty in the afternoon and are "at work" from then until after the game.

But everyone else that works for the club has been at work for seven or eight hours by that time. As far as the fans are concerned, that goes pretty much unnoticed, I think.

Our office hours begin officially at nine-thirty in the morning. We're here until after the game is over. If we happen to have played eighteen innings the night before, our office hours still begin at nine-thirty A.M.

What days do you have off during the season?

The players aren't permitted to play more than nineteen days in a row. That's in the contract that the Players' Association has with organized baseball. After nineteen days, they have to have an off day. They don't have to come to the stadium. They don't have to practice. But the Yankee offices are still open. I'm still here at nine-thirty in the morning. So are the people who work for me. There are no off days for us.

In baseball, we're all collectively devoted to such a degree that it's kind of masochistic. It's a difficult business to be in.

What about the off-season? Do things ease up then?

In this job, you're on call twenty-four hours a day, three hundred sixty-five days a year.

What happens during the off-season is that instead of working from nine-thirty in the morning until eleven-thirty or midnight, we only work from nine-thirty in the morning until six or six-thirty. In other words, we cut back to schedules that other people consider normal.

Many high school students have the ambition of working for a professional baseball team. What kind of training or schooling should they seek?

I got this job because of a fluke. A lady friend of mine is the reason I'm in baseball. She was Bill Guilfoile's neighbor in Bethel Park, Pennsylvania, and Guilfoile was the director of public relations for the Pittsburgh Pirates.

This lady was the bridesmaid at the wedding at which I was the best man of a good friend of mine. I met her. She made the contact with Bill Guilfoile. Guilfoile asked me to come and intern. I interned with the Pirates for six months. Later I was named his assistant. I was his assistant for two years. Then, I was the head guy for four years.

There's a similar pattern concerning almost everyone else's existence in this business. It's a matter of being in the right place at the right time.

But isn't college training important?

I'm glad I spent my life from age seventeen through age twenty-two getting a college education. The maturation process was wonderful. But through unavoidable circumstances they never taught me anything in college that has ever come into play in professional baseball.

The essential qualification for this job is common sense. If there are any other attributes necessary, they have to do with the physical capabilities—energy and exuberance.

I have a problem with colleges that profess to prepare students to go into my line of work. It's a joke. It's a sham. You can't be trained to do this type of work by people who have never done it in an environment that cannot hope to duplicate it. The only way to learn to do it is to do it.

I don't go so far as to say to students, "Stop wasting your parents' money." But there are some realities involved. There are only twenty-six jobs like this in the world.

A student who graduates from the medical college of a university, and he's a good doctor, he's going to get to practice medicine. But a good PR person that graduates from the same university in its sports administration program is not guaranteed an opportunity. There's no demand. There's an overwhelming supply.

After being with a team constantly for several years, you must get to be a very dedicated fan.

I love the game, but I'm not a fan in the classic sense. I have friends who are very successful in other fields. They're able to be fans. It's not a business to them. Their entire approach is different than mine. I can't jump up and down and scream and yell. When I was with the Pirates and the team clinched the Eastern Division championship in 1979, I remember not showing any visible sign of satisfaction about it.

None at all?
Well, I may have had a knowing smile on my face.

·6·

Beat Writer

The definition of *beat*, according to the dictionary, is "the area regularly covered by a policeman or sentry." The person can also be a newspaper reporter.

From spring training through the play-offs, every National and American League team is covered by a number of beat writers. It can be as few as two or three (as in the case of the Atlanta Braves or Houston Astros) or as many as seven or eight (the Los Angeles Dodgers and the New York Yankees).

Most fans look upon the beat writer with envy. He gets admitted to the park free, is able to mingle with the players before and after the game, and watches the action from a choice seat. He gets to travel with the team. All his transportation and living expenses are paid for by his newspaper. What could be better than that?

The realities of the job suggest that it is not as fun-filled as the average fan believes. Yes, there are moments of drama and excitement, but there are also long stretches of monotony and boredom. A beat writer can develop friendships with the players and club officials, but the job, since it requires long stretches of separation from one's family and friends, can lead to frustration and emotional stress.

And there is plenty of work involved. A beat writer for a morning paper must write not one story every day, but three of them. Each appears in a different edition of the paper. He first has to file an "early" story, one that is based on information he gathers before the game. Second, he has to write a running story—called, simply, a "running" while the game is in progress. More or less a play-by-play account of the game, the running, along with a bulletin lead, a summary of the game's outcome, is transmitted to the paper as soon as the game is over. Third, he must write a new story, a comprehensive wrap-up, after the game. This story, which is substituted for the running and the bulletin lead, is called a "sub."

Besides the writing he must do, the beat writer is constantly gathering information before and after the game—in the clubhouses, pressroom, dugouts, around the batting cage, and while aboard the team bus or plane. He has to be relentless in his search for interesting facts and colorful anecdotes.

Moss Klein, thirty-four, from Edison, New Jersey, covers the New York Yankees as beat writer for the *Newark Star-Ledger,* one of the nation's biggest daily newspapers, with a daily circulation of 440,000 and a Sunday circulation of 650,000. He is the New York Yankee correspondent for *The Sporting News,* and also served as chairman of the New York chapter of the Baseball Writers' Association in 1983 and 1984.

Moss's older brother, Dave, covers professional football for the *Star-Ledger,* and his father, Willie, is the sports editor at the paper. "He has reached the legend stage," says Moss. "It's his fifty-third year there.

"Years ago, he covered the Newark Bears, the great minor league team of the Yankees. He was with the Bears right up until the 1940s. But he took a dislike to traveling because he wanted to spend more time with the family. He started working inside, and eventually became sports editor in 1962."

Moss remembers going to spring training with his father when he was five or six, meeting Gil Hodges, manager of the Mets, and trading comic books with Gil Hodges, Jr.

When he was growing up, Moss was constantly exposed to news writing and reporting. "My father would always come home with the newspaper—I was always a sports fan—and he used to leave it right by my bed. And he and Dave were always talking about things at the office. It just grew on me."

When Moss was in high school, he looked forward to the day when he could join his father and brother in newspaper work. He recalls that in high school typing class he used to get great enjoyment out of typing headlines on mock stories he'd written. "It seemed so exciting," he says.

But after Moss graduated from high school and began attending Rutgers University, his attitude changed. He still had the vague idea that he wanted to work on a newspaper, but he began to question just why he did. "I thought maybe I wanted to do newspaper work simply because it was something I had always known. I tried to battle against it. I purposely did not work for the Rutgers newspaper. I decided I would major in English in college and then see what I wanted to do."

Moss was still undecided about a career choice as his final year at college began. Some of his college friends were applying to law school, and although Moss had never thought seriously about becoming a lawyer, he figured that attending law school would give him something to do after he had graduated.

He applied to the University of Miami law school and was accepted. Okay, this sounds like fun, he thought. I'll go to Florida for three years. It's a beautiful school, and when I'm finished, I'll be lawyer.

Moss went to Miami and started classes. But he had no real interest in them. "I felt like I didn't belong there," he says. After only a few days, he dropped out.

Not long after, Moss's father happened to speak with Mort Pye, managing editor of the *Star-Ledger*. Pye asked how Moss was doing in Florida.

"He's doing fine," Mr. Klein said, "but he's no longer in school."

Pye asked what had happened. Mr. Klein told him that Moss had quit law school and was applying for jobs at various newspapers. He had, in fact, written to a friend in Washington and was considering going there to see whether he could get a job on *The Washington Post*.

Mort Pye said, "If he wants to work for a newspaper, why doesn't he come here and work on a trial basis?"

"Well," said Mr. Klein, "I didn't think you'd want another one."

"The first two have turned out pretty good," the managing editor said, "so we'll try him."

His father called Moss. He came home on a Monday night, went to see Mort Pye on Tuesday, and started working on a trial basis on Wednesday.

How did you happen to get assigned as a beat writer covering the Yankees?

My first writing assignments on the *Ledger* dealt with college teams. I started off covering Rutgers football and Rutgers basketball.

At the *Ledger*, they often cover teams that have national importance too, so I wound up covering some really fun games. This was during the period when UCLA was virtually unbeatable in basketball, and I covered some UCLA games, including the famous game when Notre Dame beat UCLA.

About a month before baseball spring training was going to start in 1976, Jim Ogle, who had been covering the Yankees

At Yankee spring training camp at Fort Lauderdale, Florida, Klein chats with Bucky Dent, manager of the Sarasota Yankees. (*George Sullivan*)

for many years for the paper, said he wanted to retire. I was named as his successor.

At the time, I was still covering Rutgers basketball. The team had won fourteen or fifteen games in a row. It was decided I would continue to cover the team until it lost, which would be a big story for the *Ledger*. Ogle was already in Florida and covering the Yankees in spring training.

What happened was that Rutgers continued to win, achieving a thirty-one-and-oh record. They didn't lose until the semifinals of the national NCAA tournament, which was held in Philadelphia that year.

Rutgers lost on a Saturday to Michigan and lost again in the consolation game to UCLA on Monday. On Tuesday I got a flight to Fort Lauderdale, and that began my Yankee coverage.

It was the last week of 1976 spring training. I've been with the Yankees ever since.

Did you have any problems in your first weeks with the team?

When I first started traveling with the club, I didn't enjoy road trips. I didn't know the people on the teams. I hadn't yet become friends with the other people who traveled with the team.

Also, it was a totally different life-style. When I had covered other things on the paper, such as college basketball, it was only a couple of games a week. I lived a normal life-style. I was home every night.

When I started to cover the Yankees, I was excited about it, but it was hard to stay in touch with friends who had normal jobs. I was either away or working nights. It threw me off.

In time, at least in my case, I developed friendships with other writers and people like that. My life shifted into that circle.

One advantage that I have is that a lot of my high school and college friends wound up living in American League cities. So while my job made it harder for me to stay in touch with my friends in New Jersey, I have been able to stay in touch with my friends in California, Minnesota, and those places.

What else do you remember about your first weeks with the team?

My first season with the Yankees—1976—was also Billy Martin's first as manager. I had always heard what a great manager he was. The second game of the season, the Yankees played Milwaukee. Don Money hit what everyone thought was a grand-slam home run in the bottom of the ninth inning that apparently won the game for the Brewers.

Suddenly Martin came running out onto the field to protest. What had happened was that first baseman Chris Chambliss had called time just before the pitcher had thrown to Money. The umpire had signaled time-out, but nobody had seen him. The grand slam didn't count.

The Brewers, thinking they had won, had gone into the locker room. They had to be brought back out.

This guy is really a great manager, I thought. He had a grand-slam home run wiped out.

Do you try to impart any special flavor to the stories you write?

I don't think covering baseball and the Yankees, or covering sports, in general, is like working on the news side, where you're dealing with actual life-and-death stories. A lot of people seem to treat sports in that way.

For the readers, sport is a diversion. It's something that entertains them.

People that I talk to and friends of mine don't really enjoy their jobs that much. A job is something you have to do. You look forward to when the day is over and to the weekend. It seems like sport is a great diversion. Everyone seems to get a vicarious enjoyment from following the Yankees or another team.

I try to treat it that way, even when it gets into the [George] Steinbrenner, Reggie [Jackson], and Billy [Martin] things. I look for humor in those incidents rather than treating them too seriously.

If a player is injured or has his career ruined or something like that, it's serious. But, otherwise, it's just another aspect of the entertainment field.

How many games do you cover in a season?

From the beginning of February, when I leave for spring training, to the end of October, it's strictly baseball for me. I cover an average of a hundred thirty games per season [of the 162 played]. I'll get some days off when the team is home just to break things up.

Our system is this: I cover the Yankees. Dan Castellano covers the Mets. He follows the same schedule that I do. He makes every road trip and takes some days off at home. We have third and fourth writers that cover whatever games Dan and I miss.

You've been covering the Yankees for almost ten years now. You must have developed some close friendships with many of the players.

I have—but with the Yankees one of the things that prevents that is the constant turnover the team has had over the years. It seems like when you do develop a good relationship with a player, he's usually gone within the next few months.

But can't friendships create problems for a writer? Are you able to write critically of a person you consider a friend?

I've always felt that you can be friendly with a player. And if he is your friend, then he is going to understand what your job is. The players who have had angry reactions when I've written something that's critical about them aren't my friends.

My reputation is that I'm fair. I don't go out of my way to look for something negative. If it's there, I'm honest about it. I'm not looking to sensationalize or come up with negative stories.

So I've always felt that if a player is going to get upset and be mad at me for something I know is fair, then I'm going to think less of that player.

Some of the players I've felt I've had more than the normal reporter-player relationship with over the years are Rick Cerone, Tommy John, Bucky Dent, and Chris Chambliss. More recently, I was fairly close to Goose Gossage and Graig Nettles. Whenever I wrote anything negative about them, I made sure they saw it. Most of the time there was no problem.

Most of the players who have confidence in themselves, and are at all secure, recognize that sometimes things are going to have to be written negatively about them. If, for example, Nettles makes two errors in a game, you can't say that Nettles played a good game that day.

It's the guys who are the fringe-type and, I guess, worried about their careers, who get more upended by anything that's written about them that is negative.

Do you consider yourself a fan of the Yankees?

I root for excitement. In 1978, when it got down to that play-off game, after the Yankees had made their great comeback after being so far behind [14 games], it really didn't matter to me who won. The season had been exciting. People were talking about it.

Suppose the Yankees are playing a night game at home. What time do you start work?

From where I live, in Edison, it's forty-two miles to the parking lot at Yankee Stadium. So if I leave too late, I run the danger of getting stuck in all of the massive commuter traffic jams. The George Washington Bridge is always backed up with traffic when it gets late.

Besides, I like to be around; I feel more comfortable. Over the years with the Yankees, you develop this fear of missing something. So for an eight-oh-five game, I usually leave my house between three-thirty and three-forty-five. I'm at the ballpark at five.

I kind of hang around until six or six-thirty. I spend my time between the dugout, the manager's office, and the locker room, talking to the manager and the players.

When do you do your pregame story, your early story?
Some papers have deadlines that make it necessary for the writers to do their early stories before they go to the ballpark. But my deadline is usually in the area of nine-thirty or ten. That means I have the luxury of coming to the ballpark to do my early story.

I can get a timelier story that way. If there is any development, I can write about that instead of writing about something that happened the day before.

About six or six-thirty I go back into the pressroom and write whatever story I've gathered. If the other team has come in— the Orioles, the Tigers, or whoever—I might do my early story about the other team, just as a break from the Yankees.

I do my story and then have something to eat in the pressroom. I go up to the press box around eight.

And then once the game begins, you do your running story?
That's right. As a writer for a morning paper, I have to do a running. But instead of making it simply a recitation of how the runs are scored, I try to have a little fun with it. I try to make comments about the players who are involved in the scoring.

And I try to do a lot of notes at the end—little anecdotes

or interesting statistics. The note part is called "Extra Bases." Jim Ogle used to do "Yankee Doodles."

A lot of people have told me that they read the beginning of the story and then go down to the notes. They know there will be some interesting things there.

By the seventh inning or the top of the eighth, I have the running story finished, with the notes. But, of course, that depends on how the game is going. If one team is way ahead, if the Yankees are winning eleven to one, for example, I know I can even start my story—write the bulletin lead—because the outcome of the game is not likely to change.

When the score is tied in the late innings, you know the account of how the go-ahead run is scored is going to be put in at the top of the story—in the bulletin lead.

How do you transmit your story to the paper?
I do my writing on a machine called a Teleram, which is just like a word processor. With the coupler I have, I can use a standard telephone line to link the machine to the computer at the paper.

It's a lot different than in the days of the typewriter. With the Teleram, I can hit certain buttons and move paragraphs around. I can juggle things. It's easier to make changes. You can do a much smoother story.

So as the last out is being made, I'm dialing my number and sending the story to the computer. Once I get confirmation that it's been received, I pack up my machine, drop everything off in the pressroom, and go into the locker rooms and prepare to write the sub-story.

What is the sub-story like?
I start from scratch. I try to cover both locker rooms, getting

quotes. The only thing I ever retain from the running-bulletin lead story are some of the notes, the ones that weren't affected by the game.

If it's an average game, ending at ten-forty-five or eleven, I'm usually finished with the sub-story at around twelve-forty-five or so. I get home around two—in time for the ESPN Sports Center. I enjoy watching the highlights of other games.

What about when the team travels? Are things different then?

The deadlines are the same on road trips. But I'm much closer to the ballpark. The hotels are rarely more than ten minutes away. So most of the time, I just go on the team bus to the park. Again, I like to get there early.

With the Yankees being so active in the trading market over the years, there is an ex-Yankee player, coach, or manager in almost every opposing locker room. I usually try to stop in and visit with him, especially if it's someone with whom I was friendly. The ex-Yankees are the ones that most enjoy hearing the recent stories about the team. A lot of guys, I think, depend on me to keep them up-to-date on all the latest Yankee gossip.

When you travel, do you share a room?

No; you have a single room.

I've always thought of the life of covering baseball on the road as being an extension of college, which I enjoyed. You can look at it this way: Instead of going to classes, you go to the game. After you went to classes in college, you had your homework to do. Here you do your "homework"—your story—immediately.

And the hotel on the road becomes like the college dorm.

With the Yankees, the hotel rooms are blocked out, so the writers and broadcasters are on one floor, next door to one another. So it's like one big dormitory in the hotel. You just wander around.

In your day-to-day coverage of the team, do you have any conflicts with television reporters or broadcasters?

I don't. There may be those who do. There are several writers who get upset if a great many TV people are in the locker room, and wires and cameras are everywhere, and people are bumping into each other, and things like that.

But I'm kind of easygoing about it. I figure that they have their jobs to do, just as we have our jobs to do. And as long as no one is intentionally interfering with me, I don't have any real problem with them.

I know that it is the responsibility of the Baseball Writers' Association of America to provide the official scorer for each game. How often do you serve as official scorer?

I did it for one game. They were really stuck. The other guys who were eligible to be scorers weren't going to be there, so I agreed to do it.

But that was it. There's too much of a conflict. Because I'm doing my running story during the game, it makes it almost impossible to do a good job as a scorer.

Maybe if I had a different deadline, where I could sit and watch the game carefully, I'd think differently about it. But I'd hate to be guilty of looking down at my machine and writing and the ball is hit and the third baseman bobbles it, and you're not sure whether it's a hit or error. You've got to depend on someone else to tell you what it was.

Besides, scoring is something that the players take very

personally. A decision you make as the scorer can ruin a guy's earned run average. Or you can wind up jeopardizing your relationship with a player because you had to give him an error.

Scorers get paid fifty dollars a game. Considering the number of games I'm at, I certainly wouldn't mind getting the money. But that's not of primary importance. There's enough to do at a game as it is without getting involved in scoring.

How is your work schedule affected when you're covering the Yankees at spring training?

Spring training is probably one of the most enjoyable times of the year. It's always nice in Fort Lauderdale. And you're leaving the winter behind. But it's also a little frustrating because you're in this beautiful climate, and there are so many things to do, yet you have to work every day.

The first weeks of camp are the workout period. I have to be at the ballpark at nine or a little after. I hang around all day and either write my story at the ballpark or I go back to the hotel room or apartment to write. By the time I'm finished, the whole day is gone.

Then the exhibition games start. The games take longer than during the regular season because they're making so many changes. And anytime there's a game in another city, there's travel time involved.

It's like you're at a nice place but you don't get full use of it. It gets to be a little bit of a grind sometimes.

Do you hear from young people who have an interest in becoming journalists?

I get a lot of letters from sophomores and juniors in high school. They tell me that they want to do what I'm doing.

They want to know how to go about getting this type of job.

Among the writers, we always joke about how people think we're doing these glamourous jobs. When you're actually doing it, it's not quite so glamourous. I mean, you're making flights at three o'clock in the morning and winding up in a hotel room in Cleveland. And you're away from home a lot. The glamour is for people who are looking in on it, not for the people who are doing it.

That's one of the things I point out in my letters. I say that I happen to really love my job. But that not everybody would like it. I'm not trying to discourage them, but only get them to understand the things that are involved.

I also tell them that just by getting a job on a newspaper, you're not guaranteed you're going to get exactly the kind of job you want. In my case, things fell in place and I wound up covering the Yankees. It happened that I was the person eligible for the assignment when Jim Ogle quit. If Jim Ogle had quit a year earlier or a year later, I probably would be covering the National Basketball Association today.

So I point out to kids that you're not necessarily going to wind up covering the Yankees just because you want to cover the Yankees. I tell them my job is working for a newspaper. I just happen to cover the Yankees.

What do you advise students as far as journalism schools are concerned?

At the *Ledger*, the hiring process involves going over resumés and the letters people write, and then they call in people for tryouts. Whether a person went to journalism school is not significantly weighed. And at other papers I know about, what a person can do is more important than whether he or she has a journalism degree.

You don't have to have gone to journalism school. But it doesn't hurt to have done it.

What else do you tell students?

I advise them to work for their school paper, to go to college. Work for the college paper. If possible, get a summer job at a newspaper. Then, when your college years are coming to an end, think seriously about whether this is what you want to do.

Be sure to keep an open mind, I tell them. Don't look past other opportunities just because you dream of working for a newspaper. And I tell them my story of how I wound up being a sportswriter after I went to law school.

CHAPTER

•7•

Broadcaster

Frank Messer has earned recognition as one of baseball's finest play-by-play announcers. From North Carolina but now a Florida resident, the tall and amiable Messer joined the Yankee broadcast team in 1968 after four years with the Baltimore Orioles.

Frank got his first broadcasting job in 1946, just after he had come out of the Marine Corps following World War II. He was attending Asheville-Biltmore Junior College in Asheville, North Carolina, at the time. (It's now known as the University of North Carolina at Asheville.) The college tried to help war veterans find part-time work. Every day a list of available jobs was posted on a campus bulletin board.

One day Frank saw a listing for an announcing job at station WWNC. He was interviewed and hired. It paid eighty-five cents an hour. That was the start of his broadcasting career.

Frank became the play-by-play announcer for the Richmond Virginians in 1954. He worked for eighteen years as a minor league broadcaster before advancing to a major league job— with the Orioles. Frank says: "I've had a lot of youngsters who are already in broadcasting ask me how they should go about getting a broadcasting job on the major league level. Be patient, I tell them. You just don't walk in off the street."

Yankee games have been broadcast on radio since 1938. WABC in New York is currently the flagship station for the Yankee radio network. Television coverage of the games started in 1950. WPIX-TV carries the Yankee telecasts today.

Besides Messer, Yankee broadcasters include Phil Rizzuto, former Yankee shortstop and the team's sparkplug through much of the 1940s and 1950s; Bill White, whose playing career in the National League spanned thirteen seasons; and Spencer Ross and John Gordon.

When does the baseball season begin for you?

The day that training camp opens. I live in Deerfield Beach, which is only a twenty- or thirty-minute drive from Fort Lauderdale, where the Yankees train. I go down nearly every day. We usually broadcast all but two or three of the exhibition games.

I enjoy spring training. It's a very informal time. You get closer to the players. A lot of fans from New York come down. It's fun to sit in the stands and talk with them.

Do you have a philosophy about broadcasting? What do you try to accomplish when you go before the microphone?

Many years ago, when I first started doing play-by-play— and I'm talking now about football, before the first network football game I did—I was nervous and probably a little scared. I called a broadcaster I had met once, a veteran broadcaster in North Carolina, and I told him my feelings and asked him what I should do.

He said to me: "Tell the people what you see." (We're talking about radio now, remember.) "You've got to keep in mind that you are the eyes of the thousands of people who are interested in that ball game. Tell them what you see. If Johnny Jones

Messer chats with pitcher Joe Cowley before a game.
(*George Sullivan*)

runs out of his pants, you say, 'Johnny Jones ran out of his pants.' These people are seeing the ball game through your eyes."

I've always remembered that piece of advice—or at least I've tried to.

Sometimes people say to me: "I listened to the entire game last night and you didn't say anything about the argument that George Steinbrenner and Billy Martin had."

My answer to that is, "That's not my job." I've been hired as a play-by-play broadcaster. I try to describe to the people what I see from the time the game starts at eight o'clock until it's over at ten-thirty or eleven o'clock, and to make the broadcast as interesting as I possibly can.

Do you consider yourself a fan of the Yankees? Do you root for the team when you're doing a broadcast?

Of course, when you work for a ball club, you want the club to win. But I think you can be positive on behalf of your ball club without being prejudiced. If a broadcaster starts to become prejudiced, I wouldn't care to listen to him. A lot of guys get by with it, however. Harry Caray in Chicago has made himself widely known among broadcasters through his rooting for his ball club, the Cubs.

Then there's Phil Rizzuto. But Phil Rizzuto is a different type of cat. Phil has worked for the Yankees for more than forty years. People say, "Well, how does Rizzuto get by with rooting for the ball club on the air?" And I tell them, "Well, Rizzuto has worked for the Yankee ball club since 1941. He grew up with it. It's the only job he's ever had. He's different."

Is broadcasting in New York different from broadcasting in Seattle or Milwaukee or some other city?

Oh, yes, very definitely. For one thing the fans in New York are much more knowledgeable, especially the young fans. This is because New York is a two-team city, and the fans are exposed to baseball on television every day. In Baltimore and Minneapolis, they televise perhaps forty games a year. And in most other cities, there's a limitation on the number of games telecast. But in New York, if the Yankees aren't being televised, the Mets are.

Suppose the Yankees are playing a home game at night. How does the day unfold for you?

It's about a thirty-minute drive to the ballpark from the home I rent in New Jersey during the season, so for a night game I leave home before five o'clock. I try to be at the Stadium at five-thirty. That's two and a half hours ahead of time.

I first check for mail that might have come in that day. Then I visit the Yankee clubhouse and the visitors' clubhouse, especially if it's the first day the visitors are in, the first day of a series. I chat with the players and manager.

Instead of going to every player, I pick out three or four players on each visiting club, players that really trust me and whom I trust, and I talk to them. I can get from them pretty much of a rundown on what their club has been doing recently, who is hurt, who is going good, and who isn't.

A guy will say, for example, you should have seen the catch that so-and-so made last night against Reggie Jackson, or the throw that so-and-so made to nail Todd Cruz at home plate. Little things like that. Then, on the air, when the guy comes up, or when you're talking about the guy in the field, I refer to the conversation and say, "I didn't happen to see it, but I'm told so-and-so made an astonishing throw last night to get Todd Cruz on a play at home." Something like that.

I always ask the players with whom I talk whether the information they give me is on or off the record—to be sure I can use it on the air.

I'll spend, say, an hour or an hour and a half between the two clubhouses and on the field around the batting cage, just listening, chatting, and renewing acquaintances.

Then I usually have a quick snack in the pressroom before sitting down with the day's notes, which are furnished by Joe Safety, or the public relations director in whatever city we happen to be visiting. I go through the notes.

As soon as the lineup is posted, I write it down and make a note or two about each player in the starting lineup. The statistics—the batting averages, earned run averages, home runs, RBIs—are furnished on a statistics sheet. I don't have to keep those myself.

I like to keep a little book of individual notes that list any outstanding game any visiting player might have had against the Yankees earlier in the year. If it's the second or third time we're seeing a club that year, I'll go back and check my scorecards from the previous series—just as a memory refresher—on what may have happened in those games that would have a bearing on the current series.

I'll also talk to the visiting writers and broadcasters. We have a little bull session. I'll ask them how their club is going and they'll ask me how our club is going.

I find out whether the visiting club has brought up any new players recently. If there's a player I'm not familiar with, I first of all make sure that I have his name correctly. I'll get the pronunciation of his name from one of the visiting broadcasters.

One other thing. Nearly every night at the Stadium, the broadcasters are asked to appear before a group of sponsors and spend fifteen or twenty minutes with them. You go in, say hello, pose for pictures, and sign autographs.

It's not a burden to do, in fact, it's sometimes interesting. You get to sit down with the people who are, in essence, paying your salary, and get some of their opinions about the broadcasts, the ball club, or whatever.

Do you feel your broadcasts and telecasts have any special quality to them?

I like to delve into the off-the-field activities of the players during my broadcasts, the positive things they do. For example, Dwight Evans in Boston. He has two young children who are "special." They're not ordinary. As a result, he's devoted a great deal of time off the field to working with kids in the Boston area.

Ron Guidry of the Yankees is another example. He devotes many, many hours off the field to working with the Special Olympics. Guidry happens to have a younger brother who is involved in the Special Olympics as a participant.

There are players who are involved with the Leukemia Society of America and the Emphysema Control Campaign and things like that. I think people should know that. We hear so much about this or that player being involved in drugs or things. I don't think we hear enough about the positive things that ballplayers do.

I know how important it is that you keep score, that you have a complete and detailed story of the game in front of you at all times. Do you have any particular scoring system?

The four of us that do the broadcasts—Phil Rizzuto, Bill White, John Gordon, and myself—all score the games, and each of us uses a different method. I really can't recall where I learned the system that I use, it's been so long.

Phil learned his under former Yankee broadcaster Mel Allen, who had his own system. Bill uses a method he picked up from a recent book that relies on swirls and pyramids and other unusual symbols. John Gordon has still another system.

I can read Phil's scorebook and he can read mine. But I have trouble reading Bill White's.

Is there any particular difficulty in doing a radio broadcast one inning and switching to television commentary the next, or in going from television to radio?

Whenever you go from radio to television, you have a tendency to talk too much, to provide more detail than is necessary. This is a problem for only the first half-inning or so.

Switching from television to radio presents another problem. In the radio booth, we now have a television monitor, so you have to discipline yourself *not* to report what's happening on the monitor—as you do when you're doing a telecast.

The monitor gives us the advantage of being able to watch an instant replay, whether it happens to be controversial or not. Any close play. I sometimes watch the replay just to get a situation straightened out in my own mind.

I realize that the people listening—the man driving home on the Long Island Expressway, for instance—can't see what I'm seeing, so I explain I'm referring to the monitor we have in the booth.

I once read an interview with Ernie Harwell, the broadcaster for the Detroit Tigers, in which he named a hit with the bases loaded, and the long fly ball that might or might not be a home run, as the most difficult plays to call. Do you agree with that?

In the case of a hit with the bases loaded, Ernie has a point there. You have three base runners to follow and the flight and handling of the baseball.

In the case of the long fly that is a potential home run, I call it just the way it develops. If it's a fair fly ball and it's questionable, I'll say, "Is it far enough?" or "Is it deep enough?" And the answer is "Yes" or "No." A guy sitting in the stands is thinking the same thing.

If there's a doubt as to whether it's fair or foul, I'll say, "Foul ball." If it stays a fair, I say, "Home run!"

What about when you broadcast road games? Does the traveling cause you any special problems?

Not at all. To a great extent, it's easier on the road than at home. Everything is regimented. I travel with the ball club. You get on the bus at five o'clock. You go to the ballpark. You broadcast the game. Forty-five minutes after the game, you get back on the bus and are returned to the hotel. You don't have to pick up any suitcases; you don't have to worry about reservations or anything like that. Everything is done for you.

What do you do after the last out is made?

I have a twenty-minute wrap-up show to do on radio. For this, the producer selects tape-recorded highlights of the game. There may be only two or three of them or as many as six or eight, depending on the game itself. Then I introduce each play by means of a re-creation I do by reading my scorecard.

I'm also the anchor man for the postgame dugout interview show that John Gordon does. We follow that with a show that reports on all the other games, giving scores and highlights, plus an update of the standings.

If there was a controversial play during the game, one of us may go to the umpire's room and ask for a clarification, which we use the next day. Or if there has been an exceptional play, we'll try to go to the player or players involved for background and quotes, also to use the next day.

After that, I'm through.

CHAPTER

·8·

Director of
Message Board Operations

If you've ever seen a film depicting a baseball game of the 1930s or 1940s, you may have noticed some differences in the game. Of course, there were three strikes and you're out, three outs per team per inning, and nine innings to a game. But things weren't exactly the same as they are today.

One oddity that's easy to spot is the gloves lying on the field. Fielders never used to carry their gloves into the dugout after an inning. The outfielders would leave their gloves in the outfield, while the infielders would toss theirs somewhere just beyond the dirt portion of the infield.

Although the gloves represented something of a hazard to any player chasing a fly ball, it wasn't until 1953 that this practice was abolished.

Another change that's fairly easy to spot has to do with uniforms. In 1960, Bill Veeck, who then owned the Chicago White Sox, decided it would benefit the fans to put each player's name on the back of his uniform. Most other teams have followed Veeck's lead.

Scoreboards have changed, too, and changed drastically. In fact, they're not even called scoreboards anymore; they're called message boards and stadium boards.

In earlier days, the scoreboard operator worked within the scoreboard itself, dropping numbered cards into slots or hanging them on hooks. A scoreboard revolution began to take place in 1959, the year that Yankee Stadium installed the first changeable message board, a lighted panel that was eight characters wide and eight lines deep. The following year Bill Veeck of the White Sox designed a scoreboard that was capable of shooting off fireworks.

The first scoreboard to project messages using animated lights was introduced at the Houston Astrodome in 1965. Yankee Stadium and Fenway Park unveiled instant-replay boards in 1976.

Diamond Vision, a computer-controlled outdoor video system, made its debut at the All-Star Game at Dodger Stadium in 1980. The many thousands of red, blue, and green electron tubes that comprise Diamond Vision's twenty-four by thirty-six-foot screen create a full-color picture that is visible even in bright daylight.

Diamond Vision, a product of Diamond Vision, Inc., and the other ballpark installations that are similar to it, are stadium boards. They can be programmed to project instant replays, plus a wide range of information.

Programming these boards and supervising their operation is something like producing and directing a television show. And much of the equipment is exactly the same as that used by the television networks.

Betsy Leesman, twenty-eight, from Hawthorne, New Jersey, is in charge of message board and stadium board operations for the New York Yankees. She joined the club in 1978, about a year after her graduation from Hofstra University (in Hempstead, New York), where she majored in health, physical education, and recreation. "My first job was to work on fan mail," she says. "When people write to the players here, we try to make sure they get a response. We have pictures available of all the players; we order them by the thousands every year. My job involved addressing and stuffing envelopes and sending them out.

"I did that for about six months and then I started working for the media relations department. I did the play-by-play [account of the game]; I worked on the media notes. During the off-season, I worked on the various publications the Yankees have—the yearbook, the media guide, and *Yankees* magazine.

"In 1981, after there had been some personnel changes, I was asked to start working on scoreboard operations. We had only one board then, and it was simple. Then in 1983, we installed Diamond Vision, and my workload doubled.

"The next year, we installed a message board outside the Stadium, adjacent to the Major Deegan Expressway. We put public service announcements or our own advertising on it.

"Scoreboard operations is a full-time job now."

How many boards do you operate?
We have Diamond Vision, of course, which is a color video board, almost like a giant TV screen. We use it primarily for instant replays, but it also has the capability of transmitting videos, that is, musical pieces and special movies.

Out toward center field, we have what we call our "major board." When a batter comes up, this board displays his batting average, home runs, and RBIs. It's also the board where we display messages and animated features.

Betsy Leesman in the scoreboard booth.
(*George Sullivan*)

We have an "out-of-town" board that displays the scores of games that are being played elsewhere.

We have a line scoreboard, one where an inning-by-inning score of the game is given, plus hits and errors.

Attached to the stands on the first and third base sides of

the field are ball-and-strike boards. They also give how many outs and how many runs there are.

I know it's not like the old days, when the operator worked from inside the scoreboard. Where are you during the game?

I'm in the scoreboard booth, which is on the loge level on the first base side of the field. It's a closed booth. We work with computers and lots of electronic equipment. In the summer, it has to be closed to keep out the heat and humidity. Otherwise, the equipment is likely to malfunction.

I've visited the booth, and I know there's an enormous amount of equipment there. Who operates it?

Electricians. I supervise the seven electricians who are in the booth.

We have one other electrician who works inside the scoreboards. If something malfunctions, he's there to repair it.

Explain some of the equipment you have and what it's used for.

Well, one piece of equipment we have is the character generator. It's a computer that we use in producing word messages, such as: BAT DAY, JUNE 16, FREE BAT FOR ALL CHILDREN 14 AND UNDER. I also use it to advertise tomorrow's game, tomorrow's pitcher, or any other message I want.

Each message is given a three-digit code number. The operator of the character generator punches in the appropriate code number and the related message appears on the screen.

We also have a piece of equipment called a frame storer. It works with a television camera. When you put a picture under the camera, you can freeze it and store it for later use. You can also use the frame storer to store videos.

How is this equipment used during a game?

Suppose we want to announce names of the opposing pitchers in the next day's game. We would, for example, use the character generator to create a message saying TOMORROW'S PITCHERS, RON GUIDRY VS. BERT BLYLEVEN.

We'd then store the message and pictures of each of the pitchers in the frame storer. This would all be available to be flashed on the screen when I wanted it.

What other equipment do you have?

The key piece of equipment is the switcher, the master control. All of the other machines run into the switcher. The guy who operates the switcher actually puts everything up onto the board.

Since baseball's earliest days, scoreboards have always reported balls, strikes, and outs. How is that handled today?

Part of the scoreboard control system. Switcher is in foreground; to the left, the frame storer.
(*New York Yankees*)

One gentleman is in charge of that. He simply watches the umpire and, with the controls he has, puts up the number of balls and strikes. After the batter makes an out or reaches base, he clears the board and starts over.

It gets very monotonous at times. When you go to the ball game, think of how many pitches you miss because you want to grab a hot dog or something. Well, this guy can't miss a single pitch. When he does, everybody knows about it. The umpire looks up, and the board says one ball and two strikes when it should be two balls and two strikes. Then the umpire starts waving to get us to correct it.

The players watch the scoreboard, too. If we're wrong, we hear about it. Suppose the board says two and one, and it's really two and two, but the guy at the plate thinks that it is two and one and takes the next pitch. It's a strike, and he's called out. Well, we're in hot water.

Who do you hear from?
The manager. Sometimes he'll kid me and say, "Your balls and strikes are always off"—which is a little bit of an exaggeration. But some complaining is justified. You see, we're not right behind the umpire, as we should be. We're off to one side.

In addition, there are three or four umpires who aren't clear with their strike calls. You don't always see their arms go up. So sometimes we may not know whether a pitch is a ball or a strike.

When that happens, I'll get the binoculars and focus on the umpire's hands. Sooner or later he'll realize that the scoreboard is wrong, and put up his fingers to correct it.

You also operate two TV cameras during the game, don't you?

That's right. One is down near the Yankee dugout, while the other is behind home plate. They're linked to our video recorders. From camera feeds, we get our instant replays.

If there's a great play, we like to show it on instant replay. We don't want a fan saying, "If I were home watching the game on television, I'd be able to see that play again." Well, you don't have to be at home. Come here; we'll show it to you.

We also put the fans on camera—so they can see themselves on Diamond Vision. They like that. They laugh, they wave.

Considering all of the different types of equipment you have that are capable of transmitting images of one kind or another, how do you get everything that appears on the various boards to fall into the right place?

I do a log, a detailed instruction sheet of what each machine should transmit before and during the game. It's the first thing I do when I come to work in the morning. Each of the equipment operators gets a copy of the log. Then each guy knows when to transmit what.

In the case of a game that begins at eight-oh-five, the Diamond Vision log that covers the pregame programming looks like this. [CG is the abbreviation for character generator; FS, for frame storer; and VTS, video tape with sound.]

6:00 PM–6:15 P.M.	*CG*—Welcome to Yankee Stadium
6:15 PM–6:20 P.M.	*FS*—Yankees/Orioles
6:20 PM–6:25 P.M.	*FS*—Scorecard
6:25 PM–6:29 P.M.	*CG*—153—Yankees/Tigers
6:29 PM–6:33 P.M.	*FS*—Yearbook
6:33 PM–6:45 P.M.	*COMPUTER*—Leaders Sequence
6:45 PM–6:47 P.M.	*VTS*—Commercials: General Foods Intrepid
6:47 PM–7:19 P.M.	*VTS*—Film
7:19 PM–7:21 P.M.	*VTS*—Commercials: Flag Sansui

7:21 PM–7:25 P.M.	*FS*—Yankees/Red Sox
7:25 PM–7:29 P.M.	*FS*—Scorecard
7:29 PM–7:34 P.M.	*CG*—154—Fan Appreciation Day
7:34 PM–7:38 P.M.	*FS*—1025—Yankees Magazine
7:38 PM–7:47 P.M.	*COMPUTER*—Leaders Sequence
7:47 PM–7:50 P.M.	*FS*—Yankees/Orioles
7:50 PM–7:52 P.M.	LIVE CAMERA/MATTINGLY PRESENTATION
7:52 PM–7:54 P.M.	*FS*—Scorecard
7:54 PM–7:56 P.M.	*CG*—150—Yankees/Blue Jays
7:56 PM–7:58 P.M.	*CG*—Welcome to Yankee Stadium or Logo
7:58 P.M.	LIVE CAMERA ON UMPS, MANAGERS, ETC.

I also compile an inning-by-inning log for use during the game.

Sometimes you make personal announcements, don't you, as in the case of birthdays and the like? How do those come about?

A father will call up and say, "I'm bringing my son to the ball game Friday night. It's his birthday. Could you put his name on the scoreboard?" We take the boy's name, his date of birth, and his hometown, and then we'll flash a message that says: HAPPY FIFTH BIRTHDAY, JOHN SO-AND-SO, SCARSDALE, NEW YORK.

Sometimes we get as many as twenty or twenty-five birthdays for a particular day. And as more and more people see these messages, more and more people think to call and come to the park when there's a birthday in the family.

We have one gentleman in his nineties, and he comes here every year on his birthday. His name is John Downing. In 1984, he was ninety-eight. His grandson brings him to the game.

When we put his name on the scoreboard, he stands up, and we put our camera on him and his picture goes up on the board. The organist plays "Happy Birthday." Downing's a little bit of a ham and he waves. People get a kick out of it. This guy is ninety-eight years old and he's coming to Yankee games. That's great! Last year the fans gave him a standing ovation.

We don't do this for everyone. But when we get something special, we try to do something special.

What is the overall objective of all you're doing?
We want our fans to enjoy themselves at the ballpark. For example, when there's a stolen base, and time is called while the runner brushes off his uniform, we run a ten-second animated feature in which a cartoon character steals a base; it makes the fans grin.

And we try to keep the fans informed as to the players' batting averages and pitching records, and the league leaders and team standings—everything.

We want to do all we can to make everyone's visit to Yankee Stadium an enjoyable experience. We want the fans to go home saying, "We had a good time."

Of the other scoreboard operators in organized baseball, how many are women?
A good portion of them, at least half. Maybe more.

How did you get hired by the Yankees?
After I had graduated from college, I was looking for a job in communications or public relations, and I went to an employment agency in New York. The agency sent me to the Yankees. I was interviewed two or three times and I was hired.

That's a rarity, isn't it, to get a baseball job through an employment agency?

It's extremely rare. I just happened to be in the right place at the right time.

They're very careful here. You can't be starstruck. If a player comes down the hall, you can't rush up and ask him for an autograph. You can't be in awe of him.

You have to realize that he is just another Yankee employee. Otherwise, you're never going to get your job done.

But it's fun meeting the players and dealing with them. If some other people say differently, I don't believe them.

What other opportunities are there for women in organized baseball?

You find women in public relations, media relations, stadium operations, ticket operations, and all kinds of administrative jobs.

Is it a disadvantage that you never played baseball on an organized basis?

No, it's not. I've watched it so long, I understand the game just as if I did play it. I played softball, and the rules, of course, are very similar.

If I was in scouting or player development, it might be a different story. Having played the game might be helpful as far as recognizing talent is concerned. But in my position, it's not a necessity.

CHAPTER
•9•

Statistician

Baseball probably lends itself to the accumulation of statistics better than any other sport. There is very little that occurs during a game that is not recorded numerically by someone.

To cope with the great mass of numerical data games produce, each major league club has a front-office employee who is in charge of statistics. At the New York Yankees that job is held by Lou D'Ermilio, who, at twenty-five, is one of the club's youngest employees.

Lou was born and brought up in Staten Island, a borough of New York City, where he attended Curtis High School. He was sports editor of the school newspaper and played center field for the baseball team. He started college at Staten Island's Wagner College but switched to St. John's University, which has a Staten Island campus, when he found out he could major in athletic administration.

While still in college, Lou joined the Yankees as a part-time employee in the ticket department. "Part-time" referred to "part" of the year, not part of a day or week. He worked from February to the end of the baseball season, and although he sometimes was on the job as many as sixty hours a week, he was still considered a part-time employee.

Lou joined the Yankees on a full-time basis as a public relations assistant in November 1982. He had graduated from college by that time. He became the team's statistician—his official title is assistant media relations director—in February 1983.

During the season, it's Lou's job to carefully score each game and maintain daily records on each player. The statistics he compiles are used in producing the game's media notes, which he writes.

He also produces each player's cumulative statistics each day. These he enters in loose-leaf notebooks. In the book on pitchers, there is a page, or pages, on each member of the pitching staff. Each page is divided into columns as follows:

PITCHING

DATE VS.	S/R	G	GS	CG	W L S	IP	H	R	ER	HR	SH	SF	BB	HB	SO	WP	RECORD W	L	S	ERA

The pages in the book on batters have these column headings:

BATTING

DATE VS.	GM	POS	AB	R	H	2B	3B	HR	RBI	SH	SF	BB	HB	SO	SB	CS	GI DP	E	AVE

The cumulative statistics are not only used by the media, but by other members of the organization in preparing message board announcements, the daily scorecard, the team's yearbook, *Yankees* magazine, and the other publications the club produces.

What's one example of how the media make use of the statistics you compile?

A writer may have an idea that something is happening with

Lou D'Ermilio, Yankee statistician.
(*George Sullivan*)

a certain player, and he or she will ask us to confirm it. For example, a batter may begin to get hot, and a writer will ask us to go back and check the records to find out when the player's average started going up, and then determine his hits at bats during the streak.

Are the statistics you compile considered the "official" statistics?

No, not really. The official statistics for the Yankees and all other American League teams are gathered and maintained by the Sports Information Center—the SIC—in Quincy, Massachusetts. National League statistics are compiled by the Elias Sports Bureau in New York.

After a game, the official scorer completes a detailed report form, just as I do. My form, which is somewhat different from his, is telecopied to SIC immediately after the game. The official scorer's report is mailed. At some point, my report is mailed. My report and the official scorer's are compared to one another. Sometimes one party or the other makes a mistake, and corrections have to be made.

During a game, you must have to pay very close attention to what's going on.

I keep a scorebook open, and I have the SIC sheet out because I fill it out during the game so I won't have to do it afterward. When you put in a fourteen-hour day, you want to try to go home as soon as you can when the game is over.

I have the daily stat books with me in case I have to look up something during the game.

I try to see every play. I suffer when I can't. Something more urgent may need my attention, and I have to leave the press box. Then I'll have to catch up, using someone else's scorebook to bring my own up-to-date. I don't like to have to do that. I function better if I can be there to see what's going on.

You must be very skilled when it comes to scoring a game.

That's right. When I started this job, I scored the way I did when I was a kid. And it didn't cut it. Dave Szen [Director of Publications], who once had this job, helped me to improve.

Before, when a player advanced around the bases, I showed it with a series of diagonal lines [in the individual square devoted to the batter]. When the player scored, the lines formed a diamond.

I do it differently now. I place the symbols for whatever gets the batter to first base in the lower right-hand corner of the box, and so on. [In the example pictured here, the batter reached first base on an error by the second baseman, the number 4 player. He then stole second, went to third on a wild pitch, and scored on a passed ball. Lou circles the play on which the run scores so that all scoring plays can be seen at a glance.]

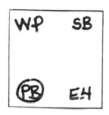

I now use small horizontal lines to indicate hits—one line [−] is a single, two lines [=] a double, three [≡] a triple, and four [≣] a home run.

Another thing I now do is indicate where a ball was hit. For instance, on a double to left field, I put a seven [the symbol for left fielder] next to the double line that indicates the double. A seven-eight means a hit that went to left center field.

Actually, it's a standard form of scoring. If I was the only one who was going to read my scorebook, I could use any scoring system I wanted. But my scorebooks have to be read by almost anyone with the club. Ten years from now, say, someone may want to go back and look at one of my scorebooks to answer a question, find out what a player did. If I used my own unique style of scoring, it would make things very difficult for anyone who might follow me.

Besides maintaining the two stat books, one for batters and one for pitchers, what other information do you keep track of?

We also compile day-by-day stats on how the team did—the game number, opponent, whether it was a home or road game, whether the team won or lost, the score, the team's cumulative record, position in the standings, games ahead or behind, the winning or losing pitcher, and the time of the game.

We also keep a daily scrapbook of game stories. This goes back to 1947. We usually clip the game story that appears in the *New York Daily News.*

We keep a box-score book which contains the daily box-score and also the league standings. If someone wants to know, for example, where the Yankees were in the standings on June 1, 1972, we consult one of the books in the series for that information.

We have press guides dating back to 1968 for all major league teams, and we have Yankee press guides going back to 1955, the year the first Yankee press guide was published. The press guides are invaluable. They give such information as ticket prices and attendance. They also contain a day-by-day record of how the team did the previous year.

When the Yankees got off to a bad start in 1984, and the Tigers kept winning and winning, all the writers who cover the Yankees wanted to know the last time that the team was behind so far so early in the season. The only place you could really find that kind of information was in the old press guides, going back and looking through them year by year.

If you have to score every game during the season and keep the stat books up-to-date, when do you get a day off?

You don't. You go nonstop. The only time I get a day off during the season is when the team is on the road over a weekend, and I don't happen to be traveling with them.

But I have a beeper. I'm on call twenty-four hours a day.

Just to give you an idea, once, during the 1984 season, we followed a ten-game home stand with a short road trip to Cleveland that I made, and that was followed by another home stand. During that period, I worked twenty-six consecutive days without a day off. And at least twenty of those days were fourteen-hour days.

You don't even ask for a day off during the season. And you're not supposed to get sick. It's frowned upon.

Do things ease up once the season is over?

The pace changes radically. It becomes more civilized. We work a regular eight- or nine-hour day, from nine-thirty to five-thirty or six o'clock.

You don't have the daily pressure to get the press notes done by six o'clock the way you do when you have a game.

During the season, I don't have lunch and sometimes I don't get a chance to eat dinner. I go to the pressroom, take a plate, put some food on it, and eat it in about ten minutes—and then I have to go back upstairs to the press box.

I can't remember a single time I was able to eat in the pressroom without getting a telephone call. It can be because of a change in the lineup, a mistake in the press notes, or somebody's credentials not being at the press gate.

During the off-season, I can take an hour for lunch. I can get home at a decent hour. I can make plans for after work.

Even though front-office jobs in baseball involve a great deal of pressure, there's enormous competition for them. What advice do you have for the high school student who has the ambition of becoming a baseball statistician?

First of all, you have to know baseball, the basics. You have to know the game.

Basic math is very important, of course, simple multiplication and division. It's not that hard.

The training in thought and logic that one gets from such high school subjects as algebra, geometry, and trigonometry are good, too. They help you to be better able to focus and concentrate.

A typing course would have helped me immensely. I'm taking typing now, two sessions a week at night, to try and improve my speed. I use a fast hunt-and-peck method. I could probably save myself an hour or two a day if I could type.

What personal qualities are necessary?

You have to be meticulous. You can't make a mistake. If you make a mistake, it is not only embarrassing for you, it can be embarrassing for the writer that you gave the information to. He's going to put it in his story or column, and maybe as many as a million and a half people are going to read it and not have it correct. That writer is going to come back to you very angry. If you keep making that same type of mistake, you won't be doing it for very long.

What colleges do you recommend for schooling in sports administration?

The program that I took at St. John's was probably as good an undergraduate program as there is. One thing about St. John's is that, being in New York, it gives you the opportunity to intern at many different places. All the professional leagues have teams in the New York area. Baseball and basketball have two, and ice hockey has three. There are also the league offices in baseball, basketball, pro football, hockey, and soccer. There is Madison Square Garden, Nassau Coliseum, and the Meadowlands complex. There are a good number of colleges and universities.

Another school that has a good program is Ohio University [in Athens, Ohio]. They have twelve-credit and fifteen-credit internships.

Do you have any other advice as far as getting hired is concerned?

One thing I did as an undergraduate was to go to baseball's winter meetings one year. In fact, four of us went—two other fellows and a young lady. The young lady was a secretary at a professional league office in New York. She didn't want to be a secretary any longer. She wanted something more challenging.

All of the owners and their key staff members attend the meetings. It's the perfect forum. The year we went, a meeting room was set aside where representatives of clubs with openings could meet with job seekers.

There are a lot of jobs available on the minor league level, in A and AA baseball, as assistant general manager of the Wichita Arrows, for example. One reason there are minor league jobs available is because they don't pay very well. A fellow who has a minor league job for a year or so may get married and then say, "Well, gee, I can't do this anymore. I can't afford it. I have to get a real job." There's always turnover. They're always looking.

A lot of kids who want to get into the sports industry should also consider starting at a college level. That's how many professional people started. It may take a little longer, but you have a lot of colleges out there that need sports information directors (SIDs) and assistant sports information directors.

These are responsible, good-paying jobs, what with the television money that has been generated by NCAA basketball and football.

I went to St. John's and I follow their basketball team very closely. When a St. John's game is telecast on NBC-TV, their sports information director is responsible for providing stats to NBC that, from a standpoint of quality and accuracy, are much the same as those I furnish NBC whenever the Yankees are featured on a "Game of the Week" telecast.

Considering the pressure you're under and the long hours you work, why do you like your job?

It's just something in me. I'd rather be busy than idle. I'd rather have too much to do than too little. It keeps my mind occupied.

And every day is a new challenge. The players play a game; it's over, and then the next day there's a new game, new challenges. Well, my job is like that. Every day is different from the day before.

My girlfriend says that I should become a garbageman or something like that. Then I'd always know what days I'd be working and what hours, and when I did work a fourteen-hour day, I could get overtime for it. But I like the pressure and everything else that goes with this job. It just suits me.

·10·

Head Grounds Keeper

To be played on a professional level, the game of baseball requires a smooth dirt infield, a carpet of grass or artificial turf, and a pitcher's mound that is ten inches above the level of the baselines. It requires an outfield fence and chalked lines to designate the batter's box and foul territory.

At Yankee Stadium, Jimmy Esposito, a mainstay with the New York team since 1960, is in charge of such matters.

Actually, Esposito and those who work for him are employees of Allied Maintenance Corporation of New York, the firm that holds the contract to provide grounds-keeping services at Yankee Stadium. It's also Jimmy's job to supervise the cleaning and maintenance of the ballpark itself—the stands, the food-service areas, offices, rest rooms—everything.

Esposito was born in Brooklyn in 1916 and grew up there. Before he joined the Yankees, he spent almost twenty years with the Dodgers, including seventeen seasons at Ebbets Field in Brooklyn. After the Dodgers jumped to the West Coast in 1958, it was Jimmy who laid out the baseball field at the Los Angeles Coliseum, where the team played until their present home at Dodger Stadium was completed. "The Coliseum wasn't just a baseball park," Jimmy recalls. "It was used for all kinds of events. On the average, we had to rip out the pitcher's mound thirteen times and replace it thirteen times during the season."

During Yankee home stands, Jimmy's day begins at about ten-thirty in the morning, and he doesn't leave the park until after the game is over, not long before midnight. "I live out in Staten Island, in Huguenot," Jimmy says. "I'm usually home at twelve-thirty or one o'clock. I'm back here the next day."

During Yankee home stands, Esposito's daily chores include laying the chalk lines and placing fresh clay on the pitcher's mound and batter's box. He insists on a special kind of clay that he imports from New Jersey. During a typical season, he uses four or five truckloads of it.

Special pains are taken with the "skin" portion of the infield. Esposito orders frequent applications of fresh topsoil that has been carefully sifted by his men.

The grass is mowed every two or three days. The outfield is cut to one and a half inches, the infield to three-quarters of an inch.

During the season, Jimmy works with a crew of seventeen or eighteen. "Plus our sweepers," he says, "guys who clean up the place at night."

"I use five people in the field," he adds. "I pick up extra people in case we get rain or something like that, to push the tarp on.

"I've got a good bunch of guys. They've been with me a long time. They all know their jobs. They know the way I like to operate, and that's the way they operate."

In maintaining the ball field, I know that rain—or the lack of it—must be a constant worry. How do you cope with problems caused by the weather?

Jimmy Esposito looks over his Yankee Stadium turf.
(*George Sullivan*)

As far as not getting rain, we have an underground system here; we have our own water tanks in the ground and the field is fitted with sprinkler heads. We can water during the night-time anytime we're having a dry spell.

What we have to watch out for is a sudden rainstorm, a thunderstorm. We have a private weather service, an outside outfit we pay for all year long. I can call them any time of the day or night and they'll give me a weather report. They're very good. They'll tell me, "Hey, Jimmy, you're going to get hit with a storm in ten or fifteen minutes, get ready for it."

When they see something coming, they call the office, and then someone upstairs calls me in the dugout, where I have a phone.

If you've got thirty thousand or forty thousand people in the ballpark, you don't want to lose that game because the tickets are already sold. So it depends on me and my crew to keep the field playable so the game won't be cancelled.

If the game has already started, I'll have my crew standing

by to put the tarp on. Because once the umpire tells me to go, we go.

Then after a ball game, or around the eighth inning or so, I'll get another weather report. If my weather guy tells me, "Jimmy, you're going to get showers during the night," I'll cover the field up.

That means I have to have a crew here in the morning to take the tarp off in case the sun comes out. Otherwise, I'm not going to have any grass left. So we've got five guys that work during the day. They do odd jobs and take the tarp off, as early as seven-thirty in the morning if the sun is out.

I read that the grounds crew at Yankee Stadium once held the record for putting a tarp down—fifty-eight seconds. What's your "secret"?

It's teamwork. What we try to teach the guys is where to go on the tarp, where to pull it, and where to stop with it.

The main thing is moving. You've got to have everybody out there at one time—and go!

Do you have drills?

Every once in a while, if I don't like the way it's going down, I'll call them out a little early, and say, "C'mon, let's go out and try this thing again."

Where are you during the game?

I'm right down by the dugout on the first base side. I have a little spot where I stay. I have a man with me. I have to be ready in case something happens. Maybe a base breaks loose or something goes wrong on the pitcher's mound or the home plate area, and the umpire wants it fixed. You've got to be around. You never know what's going to happen.

What kinds of mechanical equipment do you have?

We've got a gasoline-powered tractor that can be fitted with a front-end loader, a dozer blade, or fork-end attachments. We've got a couple of gasoline-powered carryalls that can be used for dragging the infield harrow or scraper and other odd jobs.

We've got two seventy-two-inch mowers for the outfield grass and twenty-inch mowers for the infield. We've got a three-quarter-ton, gasoline-powered roller. We've got a foul-line marker and a dyer.

I know what a foul-line marker is, but what's a dyer?

It's a twenty-five-gallon drum mounted on a pair of wheels that gets pulled behind one of the carryalls, and it sprays a mixture of water and green vegetable dye on spots where the grass is burned out. We mix it ourselves to be sure we get the color just right.

I've heard of major league fields being tailored to suit the playing characteristics of a ball team. For example, a team whose infielders aren't especially fast will order the infield grass to be cut higher than normal, to slow down a batted ball after its first bounce. Or a team with skilled bunters will doctor the base paths between home plate and first or home plate and third, tilting them inward slightly, so that bunted balls tend to roll fair. Do you do things like that?

That's one thing we *don't* do. Once the field is set up at the beginning of the year, we try to keep it that way all year long. Cutting the grass high to benefit certain players, we don't believe in that.

We keep the field the way it should be—and that's it.

During the year, you get some beefs here and beefs there

from guys, mostly after bad hops. So you go out and try to rectify it.

Most of the guys on the ball team are very good. They work with us. They tell us, "Hey, Jim, this is getting too hard," or "This is getting too soft," which is good for us.

I understand the entire field was newly sodded after the 1984 season. Tell me about that.

The outfield hadn't been sodded for four years. The field was starting to get a little beat up. It was worn out where the ball players stand. And it was starting to get a little weedy here and there.

It took one hundred nine thousand square feet of Merion Bluegrass sod. We put it down in six days.

I ordered it from the McGovern Sod Farms out on Long Island. I've been dealing with them for close to forty years.

How do you prepare for the sod?

We've got sod cutters. Each sod cutter has a blade that gets underneath the old sod and cuts it out. After we get it cut, I have a tractor that rolls the old sod up like a carpet.

I call some of the local colleges and they come and get it, and then they roll it out on their fields, and it grows right back again. When I put a new field in here, the colleges are really glad.

After we've gotten rid of the old stuff, I regrade the whole field.

When I have enough of the field ready, I'll call the sod company and say send me thirty thousand feet, and they'll come here with three loads, ten thousand feet to a load.

The sod comes in fifty-foot rolls, and all I do is hook my tractor to a roll and go.

And I have guys right behind, picking up pebbles and stuff like that. And after that, the roller goes on it and rolls it right down.

The last time we put sod down, we got a lot of warm weather after, beautiful weather. And I had to cut it twice a week.

What about the cold weather and freezing temperatures? How do they affect the field?

When the field is frozen, you can't touch it. We always hope to God we get a little snow early in the winter because the snow acts like a blanket on top of the grass; it protects it. Then when the field starts thawing in the spring, the grass comes up beautifully.

Even when weather conditions are just right and you have a nice lush growth of grass, aren't there isolated areas of the field that are troublesome for you, where there are never-ending problems?

I've been in this business a long time. When I see something that's not right, I go and fix it. I don't have any problems.

CHAPTER
· 11 ·

Clubhouse Attendants

In the dressing room, or clubhouse, along with the players, coaches, manager, trainer, and the batboys, are the clubhouse attendants. Usually there are two of them. Their duties are to keep the clubhouse clean, take messages and run errands, wash the uniforms after one game and have them ready for the next, provide the pregame and postgame meals, and pack the team's equipment and supplies for road trips.

It is a hectic job. The clubhouse men do not have one boss, but thirty or forty of them. They're often assisted by the batboys, who do most of the errand running.

The job of clubhouse attendant requires someone who doesn't mind long hours. He must arrive at the park well ahead of the players to get the clubhouse ready, and he and his partner are still at work long after everyone but the security guards have departed.

Another quality one must have is adaptability, the willingness to accommodate to the players' shifting moods. A winning streak, for example, implies a happy, boisterous clubhouse, tumult after every game. A string of losses deadens things.

Pete Sheehy is the veteran clubhouse man for the New York

Yankees. He is seventy-four years old and has been with the club since 1927. Several years ago, in honor of his long service, the Yankee clubhouse was named "The Sheehy Clubhouse."

How did you come to be hired by the Yankees?

I was a kid. I came up to the ball game. I was going to sit in the bleachers. The gate hadn't been opened. This old fellow [Fred Logan] was in charge of the clubhouse, and he asked me if I was going to the game. I said yes. Then he asked me if I wanted to save my money and give him a hand. "I don't mind," I said. So I went in and helped him.

Then, afterward, he asked me if I'd be around the next day and I said, "I'll be here." That's how it started.

I was living on East Ninety-sixth Street then. It was 1927.

Nick Priore (*left*) and Pete Sheehy in the Yankee clubhouse. (*George Sullivan*)

That 1927 team was one of the great baseball teams of all time. What do you remember about that team?

They were a hungry ball club. In those days, you didn't come up very young. You had to go down to the minors. You had to work your way up. You might have been down in the minors for three or four years. You came up gradually. You were hungry.

Babe Ruth was with that team. In fact, 1927 was the year he hit his record sixty home runs. What do you remember about him?

I liked to go out and watch batting practice. I'd be sitting on the bench, and he'd yell to me, "Petey, boy, how about a little 'bi,' kid?"

"Bi"? What's "bi"?

"Bi"—that was bicarbonate of soda, for his upset stomach. I'd have to run into the clubhouse and mix him some bicarbonate of soda.

How was your job different in those days?

You didn't wash the uniforms. You had no washing machines. After a game, you just hung them up and let them dry. And maybe once a week you sent them out and got them cleaned.

We didn't travel with the team then like we do now. No one did. We had big tray trunks. Twelve trunks, six trays to a trunk. Each tray held a player's uniform. The fella in the clubhouse in the visiting city would unpack the trunk. Everything went by railroad.

What else was different?

You had no season boxholders. Everything was gate sale.

Most of the people who came up here were from Wall Street.

But not too many people came. We used to get eight, nine, ten thousand for a game—something like that. You never opened the top deck, only on Sunday. We used to have a grounds keeper up there, and when somebody hit a foul ball he'd throw it down.

The players lived right up the street here, within walking distance of the park. Right up here, in apartments and hotels. It was a beautiful neighborhood. People who owned apartments would rent them to the players for the summer. Games started at around three o'clock. And they were mostly two-hour ball games. And since the players all lived up the street, they were able to sleep twelve or fourteen hours a night. They could eat three square meals a day. When they traveled, they went by train.

Today, everything is a rat race. Players get into a town at two or three o'clock in the morning, and then they try to sleep. They don't eat right. Everything is a rat race.

Author's note: *Pete Sheehy died in August 1985, several months after this interview was completed. "I hope the Yankees put a plaque in center field for him," said manager Billy Martin after learning of Sheehy's death. "He belongs out there, more than anybody. He was a Yankee."*

Nick Priore is the second Yankee clubhouse attendant. Before taking the job in 1965, he was the clubhouse man in the visiting team's clubhouse at Yankee Stadium. And, before that, he worked briefly for Jimmy Esposito as a member of the grounds-keeping crew. Nick was born in Brooklyn and grew up there. He now lives in Whitestone in the borough of Queens.

What time do you arrive at the ballpark during the season?
What time do you leave?

I usually arrive at about ten or ten-thirty in the morning. I get out of here at maybe two or three the next morning.

What keeps you here so late?

After the game, we clean the whole place. We do the clubhouse and the heads [bathrooms]. We do all that. It takes time. There's work involved; there really is.

What about days off?

During the season, you don't take any days off. A lot of times during the summer, somebody in the family is going to have this or that, but you can't be there. You might be in Cleveland or Detroit, or something.

What about a vacation?

When the season is over, you take off about anytime you want. So it balances out.

Keeping the uniforms clean and in good condition is an important part of your job, I know. How many sets of uniforms does each player have?

Every spring training we order two sets of uniforms for each guy, two home uniforms, two away uniforms. We use the uniforms from the year before as backups.

Each player is measured. Some guys get their uniforms tapered; other guys don't care. It wasn't like that years ago. They didn't have tailored uniforms. They just took them off the shelf. If you wore size thirty-eight pants; that was it; you got a thirty-eight.

For some guys you have to order three pairs of pants to go

with the two tops. For a big guy like Don Baylor, you have to order five pairs of pants because he rips them up when he slides.

When do the uniforms get washed?

We try to do everything after the game. We've been doing it that way for the past four or five years. Since they've gone to knit you can do that.

After we wash the uniforms, we hang them in each guy's locker. The uniform dries fast right in the locker. If you stay here until two or three o'clock in the morning, the uniforms are dry. The pockets might still be wet, but if you turn them inside out, they dry too.

What else do you do?

We make coffee. We always have things to eat. I buy things at the supermarket or the butcher shop.

The players ask for personal things. Maybe they'll give you something to mail. They'll ask you to buy things—shorts and stuff. They pay for it, of course. You order bats for them.

We take the mail every day and put it on their benches. The players handle their personal mail. But there's a fan-mail box, and what they want taken care of by the people upstairs they put in the box.

We put the pass list out. Players are allowed six free tickets—passes—for each game. Each player writes out the names of those he wants to receive passes. The list goes up to the ticket office before the game and the passes are issued.

Our organization gives out a lot of autographed baseballs to people. We put out a dozen at a time and the players sign them. We get a couple of dozen signed every day, even when we're on the road. We go through a lot of baseballs, an awful lot.

Doesn't it get a little frantic here at times?

It's all routine after a while. But sometimes when you're packing for a road game, it gets a little hectic. You have only forty-five minutes to an hour to get out of here. The batboys pack the bats. We take five or six batbags with us. The catching gear and helmets go with us. The trainer has four or five trunks.

What the players want to take, they put in their own duffel bags. We put the uniforms they're going to wear on the road in their bags.

We fly out of Newark all the time. And it's a little trip to Newark. Maybe you run into some traffic. We fly mostly charter. We very rarely fly a commercial flight. Flying a charter makes it a little bit easier.

We happen to be a ball club that carries quite a few extra people. So we have a lot more things than some clubs do. We carry a couple of BP [batting practice] pitchers with us. A videotape man goes with us and we carry that video equipment, too. It's a little more, I think, than another baseball club would carry. Sometimes we look like a football team. A football team carries a lot of trunks.

After the season is over, things must quiet down for you. What do you do then?

During the off-season, we start packing for spring training. All the stuff the players leave here, we take to Florida. It gets put into tray trunks or boxes.

There's a lot of traveling in Florida, too. Sometimes we make a trip from Fort Lauderdale to the other coast. We stay over there in a hotel for about five days. We dress out of the hotels and take buses to the park.

When we're in Fort Lauderdale, we might dress at the park, and then go on the buses dressed, to Pompano or to Miami, play the game and then come back, which is easier.

When you've been down there for seven or eight weeks, you've been there long enough.

You've been in baseball for about twenty years. Are the players different today than they used to be?

You're in an entirely different era. Players have a lot more to say than they did in the old days. The money is much, much different. No one ever dreamed that it would be like it is today, that a player would get a million dollars a year. If you said that was ever going to happen, people would say, "You gotta go to the nuthouse. You're not right." But it's happened.

What player or players stand out in your mind?

Berra. In my estimation Yogi Berra was the greatest player I've ever seen. Yogi killed you in the seventh, eighth, and ninth innings.

I remember the seventh game of the World Series in 1956, playing the Dodgers at Ebbets Field. In the first inning with a man on first, Newcombe strikes out Mantle. Yogi is the next hitter. Bang! Bedford Avenue. Home run.

The third inning, the same. Newcombe strikes Mickey out again. And the next pitch to Yogi—bang! Bedford Avenue.

You couldn't get a fastball past Yogi, especially if you threw it in his eyes. Ellie Howard said to me years after, you know, Newcombe threw that ball right between Yogi's eyes, and he still whacked it out. The harder they threw it, the harder it went out.

When he played, Berra was always two innings ahead of the other team, always thinking. He was like a manager on the field. When a pitcher started going bad, he'd signal over to Stengel to get the guy out of there, and Casey would come out and get him.

I once saw Yogi Berra make a double play at home plate. It was during a game at the Stadium in 1951. They were playing the old Saint Louis Browns. The Browns loaded the bases. John Berardino came up to bat for the Browns and chopped the ball in front of the plate. Yogi grabbed the ball, tagged Berardino, tagged the plate, tagged the umpire, tagged the batboy, tagged everyone around. He never left the batter's box. He got a double play right there.

One thing that I always admire about Yogi is that he doesn't panic. He goes along; he takes it easy.

Take 1984. Think of all the games we lost at the beginning of the year because we couldn't buy a hit. We lose two to one, three to two. I never saw the man come in once after a game and kick over anything. He'll stand by the door and say, "C'mon, we'll get 'em tomorrow. Hang in there. We'll get 'em tomorrow."